Why Policy Representation Matters

T0298724

Elections are a fundamental element of democracy, since governments are elected to reflect voter preferences. At the same time, it is inevitable that policies pursued by any government closely resemble the preferences of some citizens, while alienating others who hold different views. Previous works have examined how institutional settings facilitate or hinder policy proximity between citizens and governments. Building on their findings, this book explores a series of 'so what' questions: how and to what extent does the distance between individual and government positions affect citizens' propensity to vote, protest, believe in democracy, and even feel satisfied with their lives?

In this book, the authors use cross-national public opinion data covering 180,000 respondents from 46 countries to test theoretically grounded hypotheses on the effect of citizen–government proximity. After introducing the data (both public opinion surveys and country-level statistics) and the methodology to be used in subsequent chapters, one chapter each is devoted to how proximity or the absence thereof affects political participation, satisfaction with democracy, and personal life satisfaction. Differences in political attitudes and behaviour between electoral winners and losers, and ideological moderates and radicals, are also discussed in depth. Results of the analyses affirm the axiom *in medio stat virtus*: ideologically centrist governments are much more likely than radical ones to enhance both citizens' faith in the operation of democracy and their level of individual happiness.

Luigi Curini is Associate Professor of Political Science at the University of Milan. His research centers on the spatial theory of voting, party competition and social media analysis. His articles have appeared in, among others, the *European Journal of Political Research*, *Journal of Politics*, *British Journal of Political Science*, *West European Politics*, *Electoral Studies* and *Comparative Political Studies*.

Willy Jou is Assistant Professor at the University of Tsukuba in Japan. His research interests include public opinion, party systems, and ideology, with particular emphasis on new democracies. His articles have been published in *Asian Survey*, *British Journal of Political Science*, *Communist and Post-Communist Studies*, *Europe-Asia Studies*, *International Political Science Review*, *Party Politics*, and other peer-reviewed journals.

Vincenzo Memoli is Assistant Professor at the University of Catania. His main research interests include democracy, public attitudes and public opinion. His articles have appeared in the *Acta Politica*, *British Journal of Political Science*, *International Political Science Review*, *Governance*, *The International Journal of Press/Politics* and *West European Politics*.

Routledge-WIAS Interdisciplinary Studies
Edited by Hideaki Miyajima and Masao Suzuki,
Waseda University, Japan

Why Policy Representation Matters

The consequences of ideological proximity between citizens and their governments

Luigi Curini, Willy Jou and Vincenzo Memoli

Routledge
Taylor & Francis Group
LONDON AND NEW YORK

WIAS 早稲田大学高等研究所
Waseda Institute for Advanced Study

First published 2016 by Routledge

2 Park Square, Milton Park, Abingdon, Oxfordshire OX14 4RN
52 Vanderbilt Avenue, New York, NY 10017

Routledge is an imprint of the Taylor & Francis Group, an informa business

First issued in paperback 2019

British Library Cataloguing-in-Publication Data
A catalogue record for this book is available from the British Library

Library of Congress Cataloging-in-Publication Data

Curini, Luigi.
  Why policy representation matters : the consequences of ideological proximity between citizens and their governments / Luigi Curini, Willy Jou and Vincenzo Memoli.
    pages cm — (Routledge-WIAS interdisciplinary studies)
  1. Political participation. 2. Policy sciences. 3. Representative government and representation. 4. Ideology. I. Title.
  JF799.C87 2015
  320.6—dc23
  2014048870

ISBN: 978-0-415-85573-0 (hbk)
ISBN: 978-0-367-36603-2 (pbk)

Typeset in Times
by Apex CoVantage, LLC

Contents

Figures

Tables

Boxes

Acknowledgements

Earlier versions of Chapter 3 were presented at the COE-GLOPE II Center, Waseda University, and at the Department of Social and Political Sciences, Università degli Studi di Milano. Earlier versions of Chapter 4 were discussed at the International Political Science Association congress in Madrid (2012) and at a seminar at Waseda University. We would like to thank Airo Hino, Aiji Takana, Paolo Martelli and Robert Veszteg for their valuable comments. We also wish to thank the Waseda Institute for Advanced Study (WIAS) for providing the opportunity to write this book. We are grateful for the helpful guidance from editors of this monograph series, Professor Hideaki Miyajima, Director of WIAS and Professor Masao Suzuki, Former Associate Director of WIAS.

Luigi Curini's work was supported by the Japan Society for the Promotion of Science (JSPS), grant number S-09131 and S-12123, the Italian Ministry for Research and Higher Education, Prin 200rot. 2009TPW4NL_002, and the WIAS (Waseda Institute for Advanced Study) Visiting Fellowship 2013.

Willy Jou would like to acknowledge the International Fellowship Program for Junior Researchers at COE-GLOPE II Center (Waseda University) for providing research facilities and collaborative opportunities that launched this book project.

Introduction

Many of us are familiar with images of election night celebrations: animated crowds gathering to cheer for the winning candidates and party leaders. For one night at least, even unexciting and often derided politicians are treated as stars, their speeches commanding rapt attention and frequently interrupted with enthusiastic applauses. Notwithstanding the conventional wisdom regarding growing cynicism toward politics generally and politicians in particular, these scenes are witnessed across the world, in both old and young democracies, for parliamentary, presidential, and even regional and local elections. These occasions are a reminder that many ordinary citizens still believe that politics matters, and that elections do make a difference.

We may ask: what motivates these crowds? Leaving aside those who simply want to enjoy a big party, one likely answer would lie in expectations. Specifically, many in the crowds expect the (re-)elected government to carry out policies that they favour, whether they involve reduced taxes, more public housing, a less restrictive labour market, an end to fiscal austerity, or recognition of same-sex marriages. These expectations are not formed in a vacuum. Rather, they are derived from both promises made by the winning candidates and parties – and those by the losers too – and their past record. In other words, citizens have some (even if not very precise) idea about what policies they want, and experience the thrill of victory or the agony of defeat depending, among other things, on whether the government is likely to implement their preferred policies or not. As we will discuss in detail later, policies can be summarized by a general left-right spectrum; this is indeed a widely used measure in many countries around the world.

Since it is impractical to consult everyone's views on every issue, democracy today operates through representation, namely that citizens choose representatives to formulate policies. In most cases, policymaking authority lies primarily in the hands of the government, that is, the ruling party or coalition. This raises the important question: to what extent does the government make policies that correspond to citizens' wishes? Scholars have compared different electoral mechanisms to see which rules produce the closest match between citizens and their governments, that is which rules enhance the quality of representation (Powell 2000). The aim of this book is to take this inquiry one step further, by exploring the 'so what' question: whether and how it matters if citizens' preferred policies and those of their government are matched?

To preview the analysis in the following chapters, the short answer is: policy proximity between citizens and their government makes an important difference in their political behaviour, attitudes, and even non-political aspects of daily life. Specifically, it exerts a statistically, and often substantially, significant influence on people's propensity to engage in campaign activities, persuade others, and take part in protest, etc.; their assessment of how democracy works; and their subjective evaluation of personal well-being. Furthermore, these effects are found based on a cross-national sample that includes overall 180,000 respondents from 46 countries, and after taking into account various other factors at both individual and country levels. In short, one can be confident that these results are neither random nor based on a limited or biased sample.

Three empirical questions

Our first topic of empirical analysis is political participation. Democracy is defined as rule by the people. In practical terms, how do people express their wishes and influence policy outcomes? There are a number of mechanisms for interest articulation, ranging from casting a vote in the ballot box to taking up arms in an attempt to overthrow the government. Presumably most of us have little interest or opportunity to engage in the latter, or other means involving violent confrontation with state authorities. Thus, we classify two types of participation: (1) the conventional means of voting; (2) activities that require greater commitment of time and effort. The latter encompasses 'orthodox' channels such as persuading others about political issues, taking part in election campaigns, and contacting politicians or government officials, as well as 'heterodox' channels in the form of joining protests or demonstrations. Voting is undoubtedly an orthodox means of articulating one's preferences, but we place it in a separate category because in most democracies it is far more common, accessible, and arguably effortless than other modes of participation. Whereas all other activities listed above require some degree of interest and knowledge, the same does not have to be said about marking a ballot.

Why do people participate? One standard explanation cites the availability of resources (Verba et al. 1995). People who are endowed with more time, money, or expertise are more active participants because it is less costly for them to do so than their poorer or less educated fellow citizens. They may also have more at stake in policy outcomes. Another line of argument concentrates on people's values, or political culture. Historical legacies have fostered traditions of participation and compromise in some communities – those with higher stock of 'social capital' – while creating an emphasis on hierarchy and obedience to authority in other areas (Putnam 1993). Proponents of both theories support their argument with empirical evidence, and we do not doubt their validity. However, neither can fully account for short-term variations in levels of participation. When someone who has not previously joined any protests decides to do so, this could be due to her having more free time (e.g. retirement, unemployment), or moving to a more politically febrile neighbourhood. Other than these changes in personal circumstances, our explanation for his or her new-found activism focuses on his or her preferences on certain issues vis-à-vis the position of her government.

If we assume that opposition to a given proposal is more prone to inflame passions and encourage activism than support for it, then we can expect citizens whose issue positions are close to their government to approve its policies – but not necessarily take action to express their support, especially in political systems where the executive faces few institutional hurdles to passing and implementing proposed legislations. Instead, participation is more likely to be observed among those who disagree with government actions. In view of this, it is possible that policy proximity makes little difference with respect to voting, as both government supporters and opponents have an interest in seeing their preferred parties controlling the reins of state. In contrast, one may surmise that citizens who are dissatisfied with the government program, that is whose preferences diverge from those of the governing party or coalition, would be more motivated to convince their friends and family of the iniquity of present policies, campaign for opposition parties in order to remove incumbents from power, or take part in street protests calling on the government to rescind legislations. These are the hypotheses we set out to test in Chapter 2.

Democracy has gained wide acceptance around the world, with even authoritarian regimes making claims to democratic credentials. At the individual level, a large majority of respondents in almost every country express a favourable view when asked how they think about democracy. That said, support for democracy in principle is analytically distinct from approval of how it operates in practice (Norris 1999); opinion on the latter question is more varied. We use satisfaction with how democracy works as a measure of support for the political system. Note that there is not necessarily a contradiction between citizens endorsing the norms of democracy while criticizing its procedures and outcomes. For the most part people who feel that democracy is not working well do not want to replace it with another type of regime; rather, many of them are 'dissatisfied democrats', who are discontented because policy-making processes are not living up to the standards they expect (Klingemann 1999).

How does satisfaction with democracy relate to policy proximity between citizens and their governments? We approach this question from the perspective of electoral winners and losers, referring to voters who backed governing and opposition parties, respectively. Previous studies have examined differences between these two groups with regard to different dimensions of system support, with the unsurprising finding that winners hold a more positive view than losers (Anderson and Tverdova 2001; Banducci and Karp 2003). The importance of this topic lies in the fact that democracy often hinges on losers' consent (Anderson et al. 2005). This prompts us to explore the interaction between policy proximity and electoral winner/loser status.

Specifically, one can posit that the closer citizen preferences align with the stance of their government, the more they would feel satisfied with democracy, regardless of whether they voted for a winning or losing party in the last election. Insofar as vote choice reflects issue positions, even if a voter marks her ballot for a party that ends up in opposition, she has reason to be satisfied as long as the governing party or coalition implements policies that she supports. In contrast, some winners may find themselves disappointed if the party they voted acts contrary to their expectations. Furthermore, based on works in psychology pointing out that people discount past experiences, we also explore the dynamics of winning and losing across time in Chapter 3 by testing the hypothesis that winning gives a particularly large boost to satisfaction with democracy among those voters who were losers in the past.

Unlike the abstract idea of satisfaction with democracy, happiness is a term that we can understand and relate to much more easily. It is hardly necessary to justify why this is a pertinent topic, though it is a subject that political scientists have long neglected. Instead, studies on influences on happiness mostly feature works by economists and psychologists, for whom political factors, when considered at all, are usually used as control variables. Scholars who have paid attention to political influences concentrate on whether and how the quality of institutions affect life satisfaction (Bok 2010; Helliwell and Huang 2008). Building on their findings that institutions can make a significant difference, we extend this line of inquiry by incorporating individual-level factors, including policy proximity, and posit that it is not too far-fetched to link people's level of happiness with how close or distant their policy preferences are from the position of their government. Another way to think about policy preferences and happiness is to make a distinction between people clustered around the ideological centre ground and those who take positions toward either extreme. There is a long-standing literature on citizens with radical orientations, which identified similarities between left-wing and right-wing extremists (Rokeach 1960; Shils 1954). For example, both groups are characterized by distrust of mainstream parties and politicians, proclivity toward extralegal methods, and refusal to compromise (McClosky and Chong 1985). How would centrists and radicals differ in terms of happiness? One possibility is that radicals would be less happy because their preferred policies are almost never implemented (there are no "extreme" governments in our dataset, for example). Alternatively, one can also imagine that radicals would be happier because they harbour no doubts about, and take pride in, the correctness of their worldview, regardless of policy proximity. The task of our last empirical chapter is to disentangle the relationship between left-right self-placement, policy proximity and life satisfaction.

Summing up, a large volume of literature had established the importance of representation in democracies. The main contribution of this book is to explicitly identify, and empirically investigate, several important aspects of *how* the proximity between the positions of individual citizens and their government matters. To reiterate, policy proximity can exert a significant, and sometimes quite substantial, influence on how we engage in political activities, how we evaluate the system of government, and even how satisfied we feel about our lives. This prompts us to explore the specific mechanisms underlying these causal linkages, and also try to identify the magnitude of their effects.

In this respect, there is a well-known Latin phrase *in medio stat virtus*, meaning 'virtue lies in the middle.' If we think of policy positions along a single ideological dimension stretching from the far left to the extreme right, one can speculate whether governments located around the centre of this spectrum are more 'virtuous' in terms of enhancing political participation, faith in the operation of democracy, and individual happiness precisely because they reduce the distance between itself and a large portion of the citizenry. This is a concept worth bearing in mind as we embark on our empirical inquiry.[1]

Note

1 All data and scripts to replicate the analyses reported in each chapters are available online at http://www.socpol.unimi.it/docenti/curini/.

1 Ideological proximity: concept and measurement

Introduction

According to Robert Dahl, a leading democratic theorist, 'a key characteristic of democracy is the continued responsiveness of the government to the preferences of the people' (Dahl 1971:1). Responsiveness is one of the key indicators of the quality of democracy (Diamond and Morlino 2005), and refers to a series of links which are needed to ensure the relationship between citizens and their government. More specifically, the term 'responsiveness' denotes the government's responsibility towards the citizens to abide by its promises and the preferences expressed by the governed (see Powell 2005). In this view, public accountability and public policy, as well as representation, constitute the basic elements of institutions of democratic governance (Soroka and Wlezien 2010).

Few would disagree with the proposition that representative democracy is meaningful only insofar as political leaders act in accordance with the wants, needs and demands of citizens when they make policy (Luttbeg 1974). This does not assume that all politicians selflessly dedicate themselves to enhancing the welfare of society; it is entirely plausible that they harbour ambitions for personal power, wealth or status. But regardless of the motive, governments often end up offering policies that citizens demand in part because they don't want to be voted out of office in the next election (Ferejohn 1986). Free elections are thus an indispensable component of representation. We can imagine an authoritarian regime under which the autocrat acts benevolently toward his or her subjects and takes their preferences into account when dictating new laws, resulting in policy proximity. Yet in the absence of free elections, there is no mechanism to hold the ruler accountable to the ruled, to restrain the governing authority from ignoring the popular will.

Policy proximity is not a new idea. As long ago as half a century ago, a classical study examined the degree to which the opinions of citizens and legislators overlap with regard to social welfare policy (Miller and Stokes 1963). The focus soon shifted from individual legislators to political parties (Barnes 1977), since it is parties (especially those in government) that often determine the contents of policies. This assumes that within a given party, members are bound by both agreement over what policy proposals they should put forward and the understanding that deviating from the party line could lead to certain censures. While there are necessarily variations across countries, these assumptions of shared goals and discipline hold for most parties in democratic countries most of the time. Given this condition, political scientists have discussed a 'responsible party government model', in which voters choose between parties that offer alternative sets of policies (Dalton 1985; Thomassen 1994, 1999). We adopt this premise and treat parties as single units in our analysis.

When discussing what ordinary citizens want, it is worth making a distinction between policy proximity and simply being on the winning side in an election. In reality, these two characteristics often overlap: insofar as people consider policies when deciding how to mark their ballots (Downs 1957), we should observe closer proximity for someone who votes for a party that enters the government (what we label a 'winner') than others who vote for parties which end up in opposition (labelled 'losers'). However, we know that not all ballots are cast on the basis of policy preferences alone. This has been well established by the literature over the years, underlying the importance of factors such as 'party identification' (Budge et al. 1976; Campbell et al. 1960) and 'personalisation of politics' (Kaase 1994; Mughan 2000).

Moreover, electors not only assess candidates' and parties' positions in the policy space, but also judge their qualities by the standard of commonly shared values (Curini and Martelli 2010; Curini 2015). Stokes (1963) proposed a distinction between 'position issues' involving 'advocacy of government actions from a set of alternatives over which a distribution of voter preferences is defined', and 'valence issues', defined as 'those that merely involve the linking of the parties with some condition that is positively or negatively valued by the electorate', such as honesty, competence, etc. Also, some electoral systems provide incentives for strategic voting (Cox 1990), meaning that voters abandon their most preferred candidate or party in order to keep their least favourite alternative from winning. A voter would be a 'winner' if the party he or she votes for gains office, but we cannot take it for granted that this voter's preferences closely correspond to the new government.

Furthermore, the category of losers can encompass widely divergent groups. Imagine, for example, a social democratic party forming the new government after an election, and both the communist and far-right nationalist parties finding themselves on the opposition benches. Supporters of both latter parties would be designated 'losers', but the extent to which they would fight against the new government's proposals may not be the same, due to differences in policy proximity. Finally, voters understand that elections are not a one-off event. If past experience has taught them that, despite losing in one election, there remains a realistic chance of winning next time, then their temporary loser status may not affect their faith in democracy, while policy distance can have an impact nonetheless.

Figure 1.1 graphically presents the synopsis of this book. The main independent variable in the following chapters, namely how closely a government reflects its citizens' policy preferences, is probably not a topic that often comes up in our minds. Nevertheless, we will argue that this factor can have an impact not only

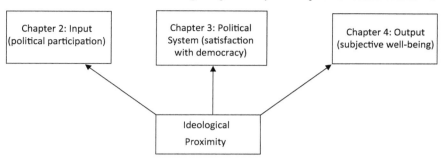

Figure 1.1 Plan of the book

when we face a choice among parties and candidates during election time, and not only when we turn our attention to political debates, but also when we try to engage in activities to make our voices heard and, perhaps more unexpectedly, when we assess how satisfied we are with daily life. In other words, the importance of policy proximity extends beyond abstract concepts of democratic representation to affect political attitudes, behaviour and personal happiness.

The discussion so far on citizen–government policy proximity, and factors that may affect it, is based on rather abstract ideas. In order to examine this concept empirically, we need a concrete means of measuring just how close or distant citizens are from their government. That is our main task in this chapter.

1.   Measuring policy positions: the left-right scale

Two pieces of information are required to ascertain the policy distance between citizens and their government: 1) the preferences of individual citizens, and 2) the position of their government. This seems so obvious as to appear almost redundant, but neither aspect is easy to measure. For example, if the government passed a new law stipulating a 5 per cent tax rise, would an advocate of a 10 per cent tax hike be considered as distant from the government as someone who wants to maintain the status quo? Since either of these preferences would change the tax rate by the same magnitude, we can say that both individuals are equally far away from the government's position. Yet it is also possible to argue that since the tax hike proponent agrees with the policy direction of the new law in principle (i.e. higher taxes), that individual is closer to the government than the individual who is averse to any change (see Macdonald et al. 1991; Rabinowitz and Macdonald 1989). Furthermore, some people who think that a 5 per cent tax increase is appropriate may disagree with the government about how the resulting revenue should be used. How to measure their policy distance?

We can imagine similar scenarios for policies on a host of other issues, all of which would demonstrate the difficulty of capturing the precise policy distance between each individual and his or her government. And such difficulty would be multiplied when we try to analyse a cross-national sample, since an issue that attracts a great deal of attention and debate in one country may be entirely irrelevant in another. This highlights the need for a common measurement that can be applied to different issue dimensions and utilized across widely disparate national contexts.

One solution – which has been widely used by political scientists over the years – is the left-right scale. Instead of being randomly distributed, views on different issues are often clustered together in systematic, predictable patterns (Hinich and Munger 1992). For instance, in many advanced industrialized countries, socially conservative attitudes are linked with disapproval of an extensive government role in the economy. While we acknowledge that not all issues may fit on the same scale, scholars have described the left-right schema as 'an amorphous vessel' that takes on meanings according to political and economic conditions in a given society (Huber and Inglehart 1995). Using the left-right spectrum has the advantages of simplicity and, of particular importance in a cross-national study, flexibility, that is being adaptable to the context of different countries at each point in time.

Usage of the labels 'left' and 'right' to describe political orientations can be traced back to the French Revolution, when the terms referred literally to where deputies sat in Parliament (Laponce 1981). With the emergence of party competition and a widening franchise in the late nineteenth and early twentieth centuries, these semantics came to encapsulate the main political conflict of that era: capital versus labour. 'Left' denoted advocacy of income redistribution to ensure greater social equality, workers' rights, regulation of business practices, and welfare for disadvantaged segments of society. In contrast, a 'rightist' stance favoured individual freedom, market competition, and limits on government intervention in the economy (Budge and Robertson 1987; Lipset 1960). In some countries such as Great Britain, this divide corresponded with a class cleavage, while in other cases such as United States, the left-right schema also incorporated a religious element.

As society evolves, new issues inevitably come to the attention of ordinary citizens and policy makers. Would this gradually make the left-right schema obsolete? Take the example of post-materialism, which emerged as citizens in advanced industrialized countries who grew up in peaceful, prosperous times came to prioritize quality-of-life goals (such as environmental protection and freedom of expression) over the pursuit of 'material' objectives. Ronald Inglehart, who developed the concept of post-materialism, maintained that the left-right schema not only encompasses traditional issues of social equality and economic distribution, but also this new dimension (Inglehart 1990). Another example involves a previously independent centre–periphery cleavage that came to align with the left-right dimension (Ray and Narud 2000). In general, scholars found that instead of becoming outdated, the left-right schema has grown beyond a reflection of the capital versus labour cleavage, absorbed other dimensions of competition, and thus retained relevance even as the contents of policy debates change over time (Fuchs and Klingemann 1989; Knutsen 1999; Sani and Sartori 1983).

As evidence that the utility of the left-right schema is not limited by the specific Western European historical and cultural background that initially gave rise to it, during the Cold War, governments in Eastern Europe, Latin America and Asia routinely employed these labels as propaganda tools against their alleged opponents both domestically and externally. While most of these countries were ruled by dictatorships, where political debate was heavily restricted or banned altogether, the usage of 'left' and 'right' in propaganda campaigns might have served to familiarize populations to these previously foreign concepts. Consequently, once these countries democratized, many citizens who grew up under authoritarian regimes were nevertheless able to judge where to place themselves along a left-right scale (McAllister and White 2007). In fact the proportion of survey respondents who could do so in these countries is not markedly lower than in established democracies (Dalton 2006).

One key reason for the widespread usage of the left-right schema is that it can accommodate both citizens with detailed preferences on specific policies, as well as those who simply want to rely on a shortcut to save them the time and effort required to gather information about where various parties or candidates stand on different issues (Holm and Robinson 1978). Even in the midst of election campaigns when we are bombarded with political advertisements, most of us do not have enough time or interest (or both) to study and analyse the proposals put forward by all contestants; it makes sense for many of us to be 'cognitive misers' (Fiske and Taylor 1991). Knowing this, parties and candidates often use labels, for example 'conservative' or 'socialist', to attract potential supporters. These descriptions, as well as party labels themselves, can serve as *heuristics* that guide voter behaviour (Kuklinski and Hurley 1994; Rahn 1993). 'Left' and 'right', plus gradations thereof (e.g. centre-left, far right), serve the same purpose of communication between parties and voters.

If spatial labels are meaningful for ordinary voters, this applies even more to political elites (i.e. parties and governments). Studies have shown that the left-right schema is related to many aspects of government, including cabinet formation and policy (Laver and Budge 1992) and public spending (Klingemann et al. 1994). Parties regularly use these labels as a marker for their positions, not least for electoral purposes (Adams 2001). Indeed, some scholars asserted that party systems throughout the world can be profiled in terms of their locations along the left-right spectrum (Sigelman and Yough 1978). It has also been shown that while party competition can take place along different issue dimensions, a multi-dimensional space can often be simplified into a uni-dimensional left-right spectrum without distortion (McDonald and Budge 2005:47).

Nevertheless, it is pertinent to ask about the degree to which people can attach some meaning to the spatial labels of 'left' and 'right'. One line of criticism focuses on the low level of sophistication among citizens, that is, their views on various policy issues are not coherently linked (Stokes 1963). People who oppose tax increases, for instance, also favour the extension of welfare benefits, without giving much thought to how the government could afford such measures in the absence of new sources of revenue. Another concern is that a person's placement on the left-right scale simply reflects his or her party affiliation, especially in countries with relatively few parties (Inglehart and Klingemann 1976; Knutsen

1997). Someone may locate himself or herself toward the left because he or she supports a leftist party, rather than the other way round.

An overlap between party identification and self-placement on the left-right was indeed common in the past, but recent trends suggest that citizens increasingly understand the spatial schema in terms of values and policies rather than parties (Fuchs and Klingemann 1989). This parallels another notable phenomenon known as de-alignment, meaning that more and more voters no longer consistently support a given party due to their socio-economic backgrounds (e.g. middle or working class) and are more likely to switch between parties from one election to the next on the basis of their issue preferences. Recognizing that they can no longer win elections by depending on their core constituencies alone, parties in turn have greater incentive to campaign through platforms on various issues rather than appeals to class or religious solidarity. These developments facilitate policy-based voting, which makes the measurement of policy distance more meaningful. A greater overlap between candidate and voters on the general left-right dimension than on specific issues has been empirically confirmed (Thomassen and Schmitt 1997).

Finally, we should emphasize that while most people may have difficulty explaining what precisely 'left' and 'right' stand for – even professional politicians do not agree on their definitions – voters do not require in-depth knowledge of all aspects encompassed by these spatial terms to utilize the schema. The left-right scale would be useful as long as voters can understand some elements associated with these labels (Fuchs and Klingemann 1989). Studies have found that even in the absence of comprehensive knowledge of what the left-right scale entails, most people can distinguish differences between parties along a variety of dimensions, which can in turn be summarized in terms of left and right (Sani 1974). This task is usually harder in new democracies where elections are contested by many recently founded parties without deep roots in society, but even in such cases, there is evidence suggesting that opinions crystallize as voters learn to understand and identify with labels of left and right (Evans and Whitefield 1998).

2.   Measuring policy proximity

As we previously discussed, two pieces of information are needed to measure policy proximity. The first one is related to the ideological (or spatial) position of the voters. We use widely utilized survey questions such as the following: 'In politics, people sometimes talk about the "left" and the "right". Where would you place yourself on a scale from 0 to 10, where 0 means the left and 10 means the right?' There may be doubts over whether some respondents grasp the contents of these spatial labels, but one advantage of the left-right schema is precisely that it does not require a comprehensive conceptualization of ideology for people to use it. Furthermore, numerous studies that rely on individual self-placements have produced meaningful results, which give us confidence in adopting this approach. One should also note that there are differences in the number of response categories: sometimes response options range from 0 to 10, and some surveys use a 1–10 scale (see Kroh 2007 on the relative merits of various formats). Nevertheless, it is possible standardize different formats, that is, to convert all the ranges to a common scale (as we will see in Chapter 4).

The second piece of information is related to the government position, and here things are a bit trickier. To measure a government's ideological position, one needs to look at the individual political parties that make up the cabinet (at least in parliamentary democracies; in presidential democracies, it is often enough to estimate the ideological position of the president if this information is available). But how can we estimate governing parties' positions?

One method of obtaining data on party policy preferences is to observe actual *political behaviour*, that is, what parties (and their representatives) do, using for example roll-call data (Poole 2005). Roll-call votes in a legislature have been analysed extensively to estimate the stances of political parties, factions and individual legislators (Clinton et al. 2004; Curini and Zucchini 2010; Hix et al. 2005; Poole 2005). There have long been discussions about the nature of such extracted dimensions derived from the roll-call scaling. At least when we focus on parliamentary rather than presidential democracies (on this point, see Laver 2006), roll-call votes measure the structure of the 'revealed spatial locations' (Hix and Jun 2009:682) instead of the underlying ideological dimension. As a consequence, what a researcher usually gets from roll-call analysis are legislator positions along a government–opposition divide (Curini and Zucchini 2012). Moreover, this method cannot be applied in contexts where there is limited or no roll-call vote data, as is the case in Japan or in Italy before 1987 when secret ballots were used in the Italian Chamber of Deputies.[1]

Alternatively, policy positions can be measured based on *content analysis* of party documents. The Comparative Manifesto Project (CMP), which analyses the pre-election policy platforms proposed by parties, coalitions and electoral cartels, represents the main example of this approach (Budge et al. 2001; Klingemann et al. 2006). After all, election programmes are a uniquely authoritative and binding public commitment to a policy position that parties make, and constitute the only medium-term plans for the whole of society regularly produced by any organization (Budge 1994: 455). As such they have an important agenda-setting role for governments and also influence the terms of the debate conveyed to voters by the media. The CMP coding procedures involve sorting all politically meaningful expressions in each party's manifesto into a group of 56 policy categories (defence, law and order, social harmony, etc.), then taking the percentages in each category as a measure of the party's priorities (Budge et al. 2001). Starting from these categories, a number of methods have been implemented in the literature to extract parties' ideological positions on a left-right scale (see Gabel and Huber 2000; Laver and Budge 1992).[2]

Finally, the third common method for estimating parties' ideological position is based on *opinions*. In other words, data on party policy preferences can be obtained from what others think and know about parties, that is through mass and experts surveys (Laver and Hunt 1992), where observers are questioned about their perceptions of parties' policy positions.[3]

The similarities (and differences) of expert and mass surveys on one hand, and the CMP, on the other, can be graphically summarized in Figure 1.2.

The coding of party manifestos and the evaluation of party positions by voters in surveys are similar in that political parties and voters are both actual actors in the *electoral process*. At the time of election, political parties propose their pledges and voters evaluate the stances of each party. In contrast, experts per se are not direct political actors in the electoral process. Instead, expert surveys and voters' evaluation share the feature of *evaluation* of party positions as both are made known through pre-determined surveys. The coding of party manifestos is different from survey-based evaluations since it is based on analysis of actual texts instead. Lastly, the coding of manifestos and expert surveys are both generated through *data collection*. As both data are collected in a uniform manner for every election, it is relatively easier to compile datasets across countries and time.

In the present book, we will use voters' perception to estimate party positions whenever data is available (see the Appendix to this chapter). Why such choice? On one hand, there are problems of face validity with party manifesto scores generated by CMP on party policies (Budge et al. 2001). More importantly, while CMP has regularly coded the content of numerous party manifestos in many countries in the post-war period, the data are mainly limited to Western countries and contain little information about parties in other parts of the world such as Asia and Latin America. Since CMP data do not allow us to test our hypotheses in countries in the latter regions which are included in our dataset, we cannot use CMP to estimate government ideological positions in this study. On the other hand, focusing on voters' rather than experts' judgement provides clear added value given the main aim of this book. Indeed, when distinct data sources are used to estimate party and voter positions separately, a 'differential item functioning problem' (see Alvarez and Nagler 2004) may emerge: that is, experts (or authors of party programs) and voters do not see the issue space in the same way. Given

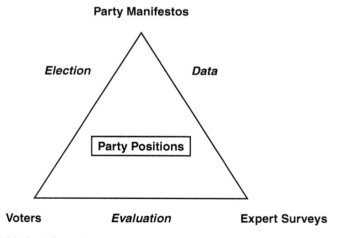

Figure 1.2 Methods for estimating party positions

that we will conduct analyses at the individual level to explain citizens' behaviour and judgement, allowing voters in each country to explicitly place their own parties seems the most reasonable solution. Therefore, we will use data on party placements along the left-right scale derived from voter responses whenever this information is available.[4]

Determining party position is just the first step to arriving at a measure of policy proximity between citizens and their government. Having determined party positions, the next step is to do the same for the entire cabinet. The position of the government in a given country is estimated as the average position of all governing parties weighted by their respective seat share. This is based on previous studies concluding that government policy positions better track the weighted mean position of cabinet parties instead of a simple average (see Warwick 2001). Using parliamentary seats as the weights is justified on two assumptions: 1) cabinet ministries are normally allocated to governing parties in proportion to the seats they hold in parliament; 2) the influence wielded by each party in government is proportional to the cabinet posts it occupies (see McDonald and Budge 2005; Powell 2000).

In the case of presidential and semi-presidential systems, we use the president's position as a measure of government ideology (unless the prime minister and the president come from different parties in a semi-presidential system, in which case we focus on the party of the prime minister to derive the government position). Where the left-right score for a winning presidential candidate is not available in the surveys, we use the score of the party which that candidate belongs to.

Now, having explained how to find or calculate all pieces of necessary information, we are finally in a position to estimate citizen–government ideological proximity. But once again, the road ahead is not straightforward. While the idea that voters are more likely to support a party that largely shares their own preferences seems intuitive, and has served as a starting point for numerous studies on voting behaviour (see Adams et al. 2005), scholars have come up with different ways to capture how much weight citizen–government ideological proximity carries. Some researchers argue that it is simply a *linear* function: for every increase of one unit in this distance, voters lose one unit's worth of benefit, or utility (Blais et al. 2001; Krämer and Rattinger 1997; Wessels and Schmitt 2008). Others propose that proximity has a greater impact, and assert a *quadratic* relationship: for every increase of one unit in ideological distance, voters lose the square term of one unit's worth of utility (Calvo and Hellwig 2011; Duch et al. 2010; Jessee 2010).

Which method comes closer to reality? Policy proximity would have greater consequences if we subscribe to the quadratic measurement. For example, in terms of election turnout, this method would predict many more voters who would not bother to go to the polls because their utility drops sharply as distance increases (Enelow and Hinich 1984). But such an assumption has not found a robust empirical confirmation yet (Thurner and Eymann 2000). Moreover, when we think intuitively, and keeping in mind that assigning specific numerical values to policy positions is a highly abstract exercise to begin with, it may be asking too much of voters to calculate their utility in complicated quadratic terms. And indeed, studies in psychology point out that human minds are better at dealing with linear than non-linear cues (Hammond and Summers 1965; Hastie and Dawes 2010). Since empirical tests of turnout and vote choice demonstrate the superiority of a linear function (Singh 2014), this is the model we will use in the following chapters.[5]

We therefore construct a measure of spatial distance (labelled 'PROXIMITY') between voters and government. This PROXIMITY variable (i.e. the spatial distance between elector i and cabinet j) is estimated as follows:[6]

$$\text{PROXIMITY}_{ij} = -\mid x_{ij} - \bar{P}_j \mid \tag{1.1},$$

where:

x_{ij} = the ideal point of elector i in country j along the left-right spectrum;

$\bar{P}_j$ = the position of cabinet j along the same left-right spectrum.

3.   A snapshot of the data

In the following chapters, we will discuss in depth the datasets we employ, the countries covered, and the size of our samples. However, here we want to present some brief snapshots on several issues to which we will return later. First of all, note that while elections take place even under dictatorships, they are meaningful only when voters' will can be freely expressed and are reflected in subsequent government formation and policies. A despot receiving 99 per cent of votes under the *façade* of a popular election, in which opposition candidates (if any are allowed) are ignored by the media and obstructed in their campaigning, and voters bribed or intimidated by official or unofficial agents of the government to cast their ballots for the incumbent, bears little relation to the concept of representation that we address in this book. Therefore our analysis only includes countries deemed free according to Freedom House at the time each election covered by the survey was held, as well as at the time of the previous election (this is necessary for a longitudinal comparison of the winner/loser effect: see Chapters 2 and 3).

Due to different variables that are needed to test the hypotheses we put forward with regard to forms of political participation, satisfaction with how democracy works and subjective well-being, two different datasets are used in this book (see the Appendix of this chapter). While details will be given in subsequent chapters, suffice it to say here that all information regarding citizens' ideological orientations are taken from cross-national surveys conducted at the individual level.

So where do citizens place themselves along the left-right spectrum in countries covered by our study? Obviously patterns vary from one nation to another, but Figure 1.3 (left panel) shows that overall we observe something close to a bell curve, or a normal distribution, with the largest concentration of respondents around the middle of the spectrum. The average value is 5.22, very close to the midpoint on a 0–10 scale. The standard deviation is 2.42, meaning that slightly more than two-thirds of all respondents are located within 2.42 points of the average value (i.e. within the range 2.80–7.66). At the same time, note that a not negligible percentage of respondents locate themselves in quite radical positions: around 17 per cent are self-placed at the two extremes of the ideological spectrum (i.e. lower than 2 or greater than 8 on a 0–10 scale). This is an important point that we will explore in each of the following chapters. The right panel of Figure 1.3 shows the average left-right placements of voters divided by countries, and shows that the ideological position of the 'average voter' is concentrated around a rather moderate value in most countries (i.e. between 4 and 6), with just a few exceptions.

What about governments? In Figure 1.4, government positions are imposed on the citizen orientations shown on Figure 1.3 (left panel). We see two notable differences between these two distributions. First, while there are citizens with

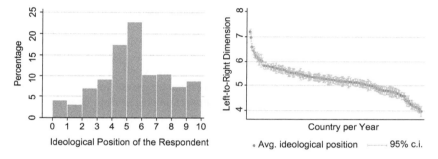

Figure 1.3 Distribution of citizens' ideological self-placements: overall (left panel) and by country (right panel)

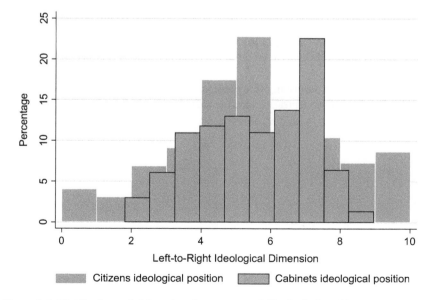

Figure 1.4 Distributions of citizens' and governments' ideological positions

radical leftist or rightist ideological positions, there are almost no governments located at either the extreme right or extreme left. Given the preferences of the most citizens, this is unsurprising. Some of us may recall news about extreme parties making electoral gains, but even the more successful radical parties rarely enter, let alone dominate, cabinets. Second, instead of a single peak in the centre, governments are more evenly distributed across a range of ideological positions. The average value is 5.53, again quite close to the midpoint of the scale, with a standard deviation of 1.57. In our sample, we have a slight preponderance of centre-right governments (i.e. 44 per cent of cabinets with an ideological position greater or equal to 6; 21 per cent lower or equal to 4).

Figure 1.5 focuses on our main explanatory variable, namely citizen–government PROXIMITY. The figure shows that, overall, most citizens are not located very far from their government, the average value of PROXIMITY being 2.25 points on an 11-point scale (standard deviation = 1.72). This is once again hardly unexpected considering what the previous two figures have shown. According to Figure 1.3, most voters are centrists. For a citizen who places himself or herself at the midpoint of the ideological scale, by definition PROXIMITY cannot exceed 5 in absolute terms even if the most extreme government possible came to power in his or her country. And as Figure 1.4 reveals, governments have not been so extreme. Also, if we focus on each single country (see Figure 1.5, right panel) the average value of PROXIMITY falls within a relatively short range.

The same logic can be illustrated in another way. Figure 1.6 depicts the relationship between a government's distance from the centre of the ideological scale as measured by the mean of its citizens' self-placements in each respective country on the x axis[7] (what we call 'Cabinet Ideological Eccentricity'), and the average value of citizen–government PROXIMITY in each county on the y axis. The graph shows that overall the larger the ideological eccentricity of a cabinet, the more negative the value of PROXIMITY becomes (correlation: −0.80). Once again, this is quite intuitive given what we already know about the distribution of citizen orientations.

Similarly, it is not surprising that there is a curvilinear relationship between the Cabinet Ideological Eccentricity variable previously discussed and the ideological

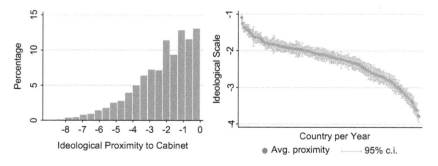

Figure 1.5 Citizen–government PROXIMITY: overall (left panel) and by country (right panel)

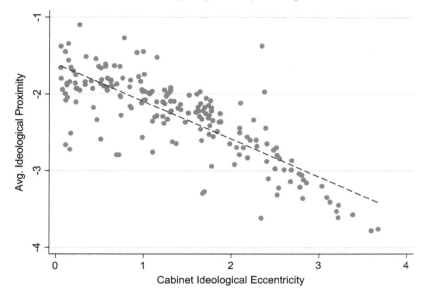

Figure 1.6 Relationship between government position and cabinet ideological eccentricity

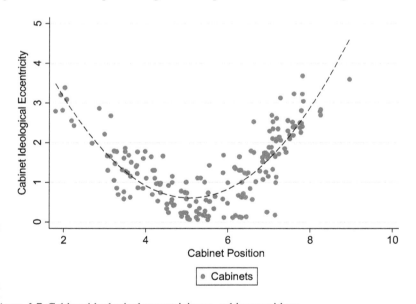

Figure 1.7 Cabinet ideological eccentricity vs. cabinet positions

position of the cabinet along the left-right scale (see Figure 1.7). Given that the average position of voters across countries is usually clustered around the middle (with very few exceptions: see Figure 1.3), the more extreme a government is, the greater its Ideological Eccentricity. We will return to the relevance of this point in the conclusion.

Having discussed both the theoretical underpinning and practical methods of measuring ideological proximity between citizens and their government, and provided a brief overview of the data, we can now proceed to our analyses. To reiterate, in contrast to most extant studies on this topic, we are interested in proximity as an independent variable, that is, how it affects various aspects of political values and behaviours. Whereas a number of previous works set out with the normative presupposition that proximity is a worthy objective, and examined factors that can contribute to its achievement, we rather explore whether and how the distance separating the ruled and their rulers have an independent impact on what we consider important aspects of individual beliefs and actions.

This empirical inquiry begins in the next chapter as we examine whether policy proximity from the government affects one's propensity to participate in different types of political activities, ranging from voting to protesting. Next, we investigate the topic of satisfaction with democracy. In addition to proximity, we will also take into account possible differences between people who supported governing and opposition parties. After that, we move on to explore the seemingly unrelated theme of subjective well-being (i.e. happiness). We will try to show that the proximity between citizens and their government does indeed exert an influence on both the input and output of the political system, as well as on a fundamental component of the system itself.

Notes

1 This does not mean that roll-call analysis is useless in parliamentary democracies. Quite the contrary, it can be very useful for example to estimate the internal cohesion of parties or governments (Snyder and Groseclose 2001).

2 As an alternative to analysing party manifestos, in recent years scholars have examined the 'contents' of legislative speeches to extract dimensions of party competition (Curini 2011). However, coding legislative speeches is necessarily time-consuming. While suitable for single-nation studies, this method poses challenges of comparability when one tries to cover a large number of countries.

3 One problems of using surveys to estimate party positions is that respondents may be influenced by their own subjective political views (Curini 2010; Merrill and Grofman 1997). Consequently, there is the risk that experts or citizens can give biased responses, and that such bias affects some parties more than others.

4 When replicating our analysis by employing expert survey data for party positions, the main findings reported in Chapters 2 and 3 are not affected. This is not surprising given the high correlation between voter and expert scores (i.e. around .80).

5 In this respect, it is also interesting to note that in all the statistical models employed in the following chapters, the linear utility function always fits better the data than the quadratic loss function.

6 We also estimate two different variants of PROXIMITY. First, we have estimated by simply averaging positions of all cabinet parties. Second, we utilize a quadratic utility function. Neither approach affects our main findings.

7 We take the average value of voters' self-placement as the measure of central tendency of the ideological scale in each given country. Considering the median rather than the mean does not change any of our conclusions.

Appendix

Summary of datasets employed in the book

	Source of Citizens' Ideological Positions	*Left-right Voters Scale*	*Source of Government Ideological Positions*	*Left-right Government Scale*	*Which Government Considered When Estimating PROXIMITY*
Chapter 2	Mass surveys (CSES)	0–10	Mass surveys	0–10	Previous government
Chapter 3	Mass surveys (CSES)	0–10	Mass surveys	0–10	Actual government
Chapter 4	Mass surveys (WVS)	1–10	Expert surveys	Different ranges	Actual government

Note: CSES = Comparative Study of Electoral Systems; WVS = World Values Survey

2 Ideological proximity and political participation

Introduction

Since the operation of democracy requires the involvement of ordinary citizens, it is not surprising that the topic of political participation has long attracted great attention from both practitioners and scholars. Conventionally, the range of political participation encompasses 'those activities by private citizens that aim at influencing the government, either by affecting the choice of government personnel or by affecting the choices made by government personnel' (Verba and Nie 1972:2). This presumes a representative model of democracy, in which the role of citizens is basically limited to influencing the composition of government personnel (Riker 1982; Schumpeter 1942). In contrast, other scholars allow a wider scope to citizens' actions, asserting that they can be directly involved in decision-making processes (Barber 1984; Gould 1988). In either case, one assumption underpinning political participation is responsiveness, which is associated with the degree to which policy makers share participants' goals and preferences. This is a point we will return to later in the chapter.

Studies on participation have mostly concentrated on two broad themes: who participates, and why do they participate. In addition to numerous single-country studies, there is also a sizeable literature dating back half a century that empirically compares political participation cross-nationally (Milbrath 1965; Milbrath and Goel 1977; Verba and Nie 1972; Verba et al. 1978). Before exploring how ideological proximity between citizens and their government may affect patterns of participation, we will first review some findings from previous studies to develop a number of hypotheses. This would also allow us to distinguish between different modes of participation. Going to a polling station to vote in a local council election, for example, is not the same as signing a petition seeking more funding for schools and hospitals in the community, or joining a demonstration demanding the removal of municipal officials seen as incompetent or corrupt. Each of these acts may produce a similar result in the end, but one can see the difference in terms of time, effort and skill required, and the likely effectiveness in securing the desired outcome. In addition, more than other methods of interest articulation, voting is governed by vastly disparate institutional rules in different countries, including laws in some countries that make it compulsory. Thus, in the following analysis, we will examine two separate forms of participation: voting and other activities.

1.   Political participation: motivations and types of actions

What motivates us to voice our opinions? To simplify, people participate 'because they have the resources and because they have the incentives to do so' (Teorell 2006:801). From the opposite perspective, one can also say that people do not participate because they cannot, they do not want to, or because nobody asked (Verba et al. 1995). More often than not, we do not mind keeping quiet when we are content with the way things are, but have reason to speak up when we would like to see some changes made. Some of these changes can bring material benefits, whereas others may involve a sense of satisfaction from doing what is 'right'. Political participation follows the same rationale: citizens who seek change are more likely to participate. Note that participation here refers mostly to what Inglehart and Klingemann (1979) labelled 'elite-challenging', rather than 'elite-directed', activities. The latter refers to activities that are usually arranged by hierarchical organizations, with the mass membership only expected to follow decisions made by a small leadership coterie. In contrast, the former is more issue specific, and predicated on some level of sophistication: 'elite-challenging action is likely to take place when one knows how to cope with elites and wants something different from what the elites want' (Inglehart and Klingemann 1979:209).

There is a long scholarly tradition linking political participation to socio-economic resources (Nie et al. 1969; Verba and Nie 1972; Verba et al. 1978), because people with more time and wealth can afford to engage in political activism with less need to worry about financial costs to their livelihood, and also since they are likely to have more at stake in policy outcomes. Another important factor lies in one's surrounding social environment, that is, influence from people one interacts with (Giles and Dantico 1982; Huckfeldt 1979; Kenny 1992). This is related to the effect of contact and recruitment (Huckfeldt and Sprague 1992). For example, regular church attendance can lead to greater political participation, not due to divine inspiration or other personal religious experiences, but simply because churches can serve a secular function of mobilization (Jones-Correa and Leal 2001). These days, it is not uncommon to read reports about church members signing petitions or joining marches in efforts to stop the legalization of homosexual marriages, and in some countries, politicians explicitly cultivate ties with religious groups to raise turnout and garner votes. Thus, one should keep in mind that political participation often takes place collectively, and even an individual act such as voting can be affected by external social influences.

It is difficult to classify whether voting is elite directed or elite challenging; some voters probably go to the polls due to urging from – and as an expression of loyalty to – political parties or candidates, while others do so out of a desire to see changes expected to improve personal and/or societal well-being. Many scholars have focused on the role of parties in mobilizing voters (Gerber and Green 2000;

Karp et al. 2008; Leighley 1995; Rosenstone and Hansen 1993), which represents an example of elite-directed participation. A long-established theory in political science, referred to as the calculus of voting (Downs 1957), posits that a citizen's decision to vote or not is a function of (1) the amount of benefits he or she derives from the victory of his or her preferred party or candidate, multiplied by (2) the likelihood that his or her vote would determine the election outcome, and minus (3) the costs of turnout (not just time but also information gathering). Ironically, this assumption of rationality is likely to lead most citizens to abstain, since the probability of their own vote being decisive is miniscule.[1] Later, an additional term was inserted into the equation, taking into account a sense of satisfaction derived from the act of voting itself (Riker and Ordeshook 1968). In other words, turnout can be motivated by not only instrumental, but also expressive reasons.

Compared with turning out to vote, other modes of participation discussed in the following call for a greater commitment of time, effort and other resources. This implies that there must be stronger incentives to motivate citizens. Note that an important cost concomitant with these activities is the need for coordination, since – unlike voting – they are collective in nature. A seminal work by Olson (1965) posits a rational choice approach to explaining collective action, namely that people weigh potential (non-excludable) benefits and (individual) costs when deciding whether they should take part or not. However, the ability of individuals to judge what is 'rational' is necessarily limited, due to constraints on the amount of information available (Simon 1985). Furthermore, many of our decisions are driven not solely by logic, but rather by what we believe in and what our friends or family do. Political participation can also result from these moral (Marwell and Ames 1979; Opp 1986) and social (Klandermans 1984; McAdam and Paulsen 1993; Opp and Gern 1993) incentives.

In addition to individual-level explanations for why people decide to participate (or not) in different types of political activities, we should also take into account institutional incentives and constraints. In other words, some systems render participation more rewarding than others, in the sense that demands made through various channels of engagement are more likely to reach policy makers. Verba et al. (1978) observes that participatory inequality, that is, the gap between citizens with abundant resources and those who are less well-endowed, varies considerably among nations, and not just due to different levels of economic development. In recent years, scholars studying cross-national differences in rates of participation have focused the impact of electoral rules and found that proportional rules and a more consensual system are related to higher turnout (Blais and Carty 1990; Lijphart 1999; Powell 2000). The same conclusion has been extended to other forms of participation as well (Karp and Banducci 2008). By giving small parties a better chance to obtain legislative representation, proportional rules encourage minority interests to be expressed through the electoral process. In contrast, a majoritarian or plurality (also known as first-past-the-post) system sets a very high bar for smaller parties to win any parliamentary seats. Consequently, small party supporters expecting their votes to be wasted may decide not to go to the polls at all.

2. How does ideology (and electoral considerations) affect political participation?

Does ideology affect citizens' propensity for different modes of political participation? And if so, what is the relationship with different types of activities?
Many scholars have examined levels of political trust (e.g. Lipset and Schneider 1987; Nye et al. 1997), and to the extent that they touched upon ideological
orientations, right-wingers are found to express greater trust in institutions than
those on the left (Devos et al. 2002). Psychologists attribute this difference to not
only value priorities, but also personality traits. A number of works dating back
to the mid-20th century associates citizens espousing right-wing ideology with
characteristics such as orderliness, rigidity, self-control, and proclivity to follow
rules (Adorno et al. 1950; Fromm 1964; Tomkins 1963), and recent studies have
empirically confirmed that self-identification with the right are indeed linked with
a need for order and lack of openness (Carney et al. 2008; Jost et al. 2007).

One example illustrating the difference between rightists and leftists is on perceptions of inequality. Citizens on the left are not only more likely to advocate
greater equality (Listhaug and Aalberg 1999), but also more sensitive to unequal
conditions (Alesina et al. 2004). In contrast, right-wingers are more inclined to
rationalize inequality (Jost et al. 2003). In turn, while inequality has a negative
effect on support for democracy, this relationship is particularly robust among
leftists (Anderson and Singer 2008). In other words, while citizens on the right
are generally more disposed to accept and justify the status quo, their leftist
counterparts are likely to seek change through political activism (van der Meer
et al. 2009). For example, analysing surveys of protest participants, Norris et al.
(2005) concluded that demonstrators are 'drawn disproportionately from the left.'
Another study also found that leftists are more prone to engage in 'aggressive
political behaviour' (Muller 1979). Moreover, so-called post-materialists – citizens who prioritize quality of life issues above the pursuit of material gains – are
more inclined to participate because they value the process of interest articulation
itself (Inglehart 1997), and most post-materialists position themselves toward the
left side of the ideological spectrum. This leads us to the following hypothesis:

Hypothesis 1 (ideological orientation hypothesis): citizens with leftist orienta-
tions are more likely to participate due to their desire to alter the status quo.

However, the relationship between ideological orientations and political participation may not simply be linear. One must take into account variations in both
value orientations and forms of participation. For example, in comparing mate-
rialists and post-materialists, Klingemann (1979:294) found that values play an
important role in explaining protest potential, but account for little variation with
respect to orthodox modes of participation. The aforementioned study by Norris et al. (2005) pointed out that it is not those on the radical left who were most
frequently found in the ranks of protestors, and distinguished between new and
old lefts (as well as new right) among the demonstrators. In another cross-national

study, Opp et al. (1995) illustrated that while there is indeed a linear increase in protest potential as one moves from right to left in Germany, in Israel and Peru, the relationship is curvilinear instead, with the highest likelihood of protesting among citizens on both extremes of the ideological scale.

In other words, differences in rates and means of participation may not only separate rightists and leftists, but also distinguish the centre from *both* ends of the ideological spectrum. Indeed, those knocking on doors to gather signatures, preparing banners for protest marches or standing on the frontline in confrontations with the police are likely citizens who are most dedicated to their values – activists holding attitudes more fervent and probably more radical than the rest of the community. In short, the more ideologically polarized citizens are, the greater their likelihood of engaging in political activities (Martin and van Deth 2007). There is no shortage of studies affirming the relationship between extremism on one hand, and campaign activities (Grant and Rudolph 2002; Miller et al. 1986; Nexon 1971) and issue advocacy (Scott and Schuman 1988; Verba and Brody 1970) on the other. Indeed, radicals' significantly greater level of participation has raised concerns about their undue influence on the democratic polity (Verba et al. 1993; West 1988).

This brings us back to the question of motives. Conventional explanations for participation concentrate on expected utility (Feather 1982; Klandermans 1984), as well as on participants' repertoire of resources (Verba et al. 1995). However, some forms of political actions can contain a mix of instrumental and expressive elements as already noted (Kaase 1990:29), which implies that, for example, people may join protests or clash with state authorities even if they do not expect to secure their desired outcome as a result of these activities. Indeed, the assertion that one function of ideology is to provide 'norms about the desirability of political violence' (Gurr 1970:194) is probably most applicable to those on both extremes of the ideological scale, where normative justifications for political participation are most readily found (Grundy and Weinstein 1974). Moreover, a more tenacious belief in their cause may render citizens who espouse radical ideas less ready to compromise. Empirical analysis indeed confirms that extremist participate more in various modes of activity, albeit not voting (van der Meer et al. 2009: 1439). It follows that:

Hypothesis 2 (ideological extremism hypothesis): citizens who place themselves toward radical ideological positions participate more due to stronger commitment to their beliefs.

Related to individuals' own ideological placement, another important element – the theme of this book – is proximity between citizen and government positions. Extending the Downsian logic from vote choice to election campaign activities (Aldrich 1983, 1995), Claassen (2007) offered evidence based on analysis of US election surveys that the effect of ideological extremism on participation can largely be attributed to proximity. Similarly, Opp et al. speculated that 'the relationship between let-right ideology and at least illegal protest may be conditioned by the ideological leanings of the parties that control the government' (1995:93). A cross-national study by van der Meer et al. specifically examined citizen–government proximity to reveal that, with respect to different means of political participation except voting, 'the larger the perceived ideological distance between a citizen and his or her government, the more likely that citizen participates politically' (2009:1447–1448). It is not difficult to grasp the logic behind this finding: as we described in Chapter 1, citizens whose ideological orientations are close to their government have little incentive to go out of their way and make their voices heard, since policy makers are likely to have promised or carried out their preferred policies already. In contrast, those who do not enjoy this propinquity may feel a need to voice their views, since the government may otherwise neglect their demands. Thus:

Hypothesis 3 (ideological proximity hypothesis): citizens who are located closer to the ideological position of their government participate less since their preferred policies are more likely to be promised or implemented already.

Related to proximity to government, another factor to take into account is whether citizens are electoral 'winners' or 'losers', referring to those who voted for governing and opposition parties, respectively. This distinction has attracted scholarly attention in recent years, and most studies show that losers profess less confidence in government (including non-political) institutions (Anderson and Tverdova 2001; Moehler 2009), and also less positive appraisals concerning how democracy works (Cho and Bratton 2006). The next chapter will address the latter theme in detail; here we concentrate on the question of how winner/loser status affects participation, in view of Anderson et al.'s assertion that losers are more likely to protest (2005:40–47). This raises the question of how to identify a citizen as 'winner' or 'loser'. A study that investigated ideological proximity concluded that 'the more one's left-right position resembles that of the government in office, the more that citizen thinks of herself or himself as a winner' (van der Meer et al. 2009:1433).

However, while ideological proximity is important for party choice, it is not the only determinant (as discussed in Chapter 1). Furthermore, government formation often occurs in the post-electoral stage, so it could happen that even if a voter's preferred party ends up in government (i.e. he or she is a 'winner'), he or she would still be far away from the government as a whole, since the voter's preferred party is allied with another, ideologically distant party. This is true since a voter only indicates a choice for a party, not necessarily a coalition that will be formed after the election. For these reasons, whenever possible, one should separate the impact of ideological proximity from that of winner/loser status, and define the latter in terms of party preference rather than in terms of ideology.

Inter alia, this distinction would also allow us to explore some intriguing interaction relationships between ideological proximity and winner/loser status. In fact, while one would expect that electoral losers are more inclined to participate than winners, it is worth keeping in mind that not all winners, and certainly not all losers, necessarily share similar policy preferences. Imagine, for example, a mainstream conservative party winning an election and forming a new government. All voters who did not cast their ballot for this party are deemed losers, but one can assume that liberal (i.e. supporters of free market) losers would have less reason to disagree with this government than communist losers. Therefore, despite the fact that in this example both liberal and communist voters are labelled losers, the incentive to participate should be larger for the latter group. In view of this, we can advance the following two hypotheses:

Hypothesis 4 (winner/loser status hypothesis): citizens who are electoral losers participate more than winners since the government is less likely to translate their preferences into policy . . .
Hypothesis 5 (winner/loser status conditional hypothesis): . . . unless the cabinet is very close to the ideal point of an electoral loser.

3.   Data and operationalization: political participation and voting

To test the relationship between ideological orientations, citizen–government proximity and electoral winner/loser status on one hand, and both voting and other forms of political participation on the other, we utilize data from the second wave of the Comparative Study of Electoral Systems (CSES), covering the years 2001–2006.[2] The CSES dataset has the advantages of employing the same battery of questions across countries, constituting the largest single source of available cases, and containing all information needed to build our variables. While there are later CSES modules with more recent data, only the second wave contains items on different modes of participation that comprise our dependent variables. Also, since our hypotheses rest on assumptions about electoral fairness and government responsiveness, only countries that are rated as 'free' by Freedom House at the time of the survey are included in the following empirical analysis (see the discussion in Chapter 1). This leaves us with 36 election surveys (covering 34 countries: see Table 2.1), including not only established Western democracies, but also new democracies in Central and Eastern Europe, Latin America and East Asia.[3] In the second column of Table 2.1, we report the time of the elections when the surveys were conducted, and in the third column, the time of the previous election (a distinction we will return to later). The type of election is reported in the fourth column.

Table 2.1 List of electoral surveys analysed in Chapter 2

Country	Current Election	Previous Election	Type of Election
Australia	2004	2001	Legislative
Belgium	2003	1999	Legislative
Brazil	2002	1998	Presidential
Bulgaria	2001	1997	Legislative
Canada	2004	2000	Legislative

Country	Current Election	Previous Election	Type of Election
Chile	2005	1999	Presidential
Czech Republic	2002	1998	Legislative
Denmark	2001	1998	Legislative
Finland	2003	1999	Legislative
France	2002	1995	Presidential
Germany	2002	1998	Legislative
Hungary	2002	1998	Legislative
Iceland	2003	1999	Legislative
Ireland	2002	1997	Legislative
Israel	2003	1999	Legislative
Italy	2006	2001	Legislative
Japan	2004*	2003	Legislative
Mexico	2003	2000	Legislative
Netherlands	2002	1998	Legislative
New Zealand	2002	1999	Legislative
Norway	2001	1996	Legislative
Peru	2006	2001	Presidential
Philippines	2004	2001	Presidential
Poland	2001	1997	Legislative
Portugal	2002	1999	Legislative
Portugal	2005	2002	Legislative
Romania	2004	2000	Presidential
Slovenia	2004	2000	Legislative
South Korea	2004	2000	Legislative
Spain	2004	2000	Legislative
Sweden	2002	1998	Legislative
Switzerland	2003	1999	Legislative
Taiwan	2001	1998	Legislative
Taiwan	2004	2000	Presidential
Great Britain	2005	2001	Legislative
United States	2004	2000	Presidential

Notes: * all legislative elections in bicameral systems refer to the lower chamber, except Japan 2004 (upper house – Japanese House of Councilors – election).

In the CSES dataset, we have information on six types of political action (see Box 2.1): *voting* (cast a ballot at the last parliamentary election); *contacting* (contacted a politician or government official during the last five years); *campaigning* (supported a particular party or candidate by, for example, attending a meeting or putting up a poster); *persuading* (talked to other people to persuade them to vote for a given party or candidate); *cooperating* (worked with others who share the same political concerns) and *protesting* (took part in a protest, march or demonstration). All six measures are dichotomous, since the most important distinction is that between those who participate and those who do not, rather than the frequency of involvement.

Box 2.1   Survey question wording for each mode of political participation

- Over the past five years or so, have you done any of the following things to express your views about something the government should or should not be doing?
  - *Contacting*: contacted a politician or government official either in person, or in writing, or some other way?
  - *Protesting*: taken part in a protest, march or demonstration?
  - *Cooperating*: worked together with people who shared the same concern?
- Here is a list of things some people do during elections. Which if any did you do during the most recent election?
  - *Persuading*: talked to other people to persuade them to vote for a particular party or candidate?
  - *Campaigning*: showed your support for a particular party or candidate by, for example, attending a meeting, putting up a poster or in some other way?

One way to investigate factors that influence participation is to examine each mode of political action separately (as done in van der Meer et al. 2009), while another common method uses a single, aggregate participation index (Bourne 2010; Dalton et al. 2010; Dawes et al. 2011; Miller et al. 1981). We follow the latter option. Specifically, we construct an additive index using an unweighted sum of yes/no responses to all of the aforementioned activities except turnout, which is analysed separately. The choice to exclude voting from our index is based on both theoretical and empirical justifications. Theoretically, our hypotheses are based on the assumption that, since activities such as contacting and campaigning require considerable time and effort, only citizens who are dedicated to changing the status quo would have incentive to become involved. In contrast, the costs of voting are lower, meaning that citizens who go to the polls are not necessarily driven by similar commitments. Thus, we do not expect ideological proximity to government to exert a notable influence on individual decisions to turn out or abstain. Voters can decide to go to the polls for reasons that are not related to policy preferences and ideological orientations, such as a sense of civic duty or an affirmation of belief in the democratic process.

The empirical justification for constructing an aggregate participation index excluding turnout derives from two complementary analyses. First, we ran a Principal Component Analysis[4] on the political activities previously discussed, first excluding and then including the voting variable. A principal components analysis is a data-reduction technique that essentially groups together sets of highly correlated variables to identify a lesser number of underlying factors that explain most of the variance in the data. When analysing the five political activities other than voting, the Principal Component Analysis yields only one eigenvalue exceeding the value of 1, which explains almost 60 per cent of all variance. In contrast, the equivalent figure is less than 50 per cent when we replicate the analysis with voting included. Furthermore, there is a second eigenvalue larger than 1 on which turnout loads more strongly than on the first one. This affirms that voting belongs to a different latent dimension from the other five activities which fit well together.[5]

A similar result stems from the application of a reliability analysis to the six types of activities included in the CSES. This analysis allows us to assess the internal consistency of a scale, meaning the degree to which the items that make up the scale 'fit together', that is, if they are all measuring the same underlying construct. One of the most commonly used indicators of internal consistency is Cronbach's alpha coefficient. Ideally, the Cronbach's alpha coefficient would exceed 0.7, but with respect to the political participation index, values around 0.6 are deemed acceptable (see Dawes et al. 2011, Flavin and Keane 2012, Marien et al. 2010). Our aggregate index has a Cronbach's alpha of 0.59, positive though not very high by the standards of the Likert attitude scale. To test whether all the indicators belong to the same scale, values for the Cronbach alpha coefficient are also computed when specific items are removed from the scale. The result shows once again that 'voting' does not tap the same conceptual dimension as the other indicators. Removing this category boosts the Cronbach alpha to a respectable 0.63 (see Table 2.2).

Summing up, we focus on two main dependent variables: (1) voting, and (2) an aggregate index of participation comprising contacting, campaigning, persuading, cooperating and protesting. For the former, respondents are coded 1 if they reported casting a ballot, and 0 otherwise. The latter ranges between 0 (a citizen has not participated in any of these activities) and 5 (a citizen has taken part in all five activities). The mean value for voting is 0.870, meaning that on average nearly 9 out of 10 respondents in our sample said they voted in the election covered by the survey. The average value for participation index is 0.801 (standard deviation: 1.15), with slightly less than 22 per cent having taken part in two or more types of activities.

Table 2.2 Cronbach's alpha for the political actions items

	Alpha = 0.59
	(column below: alpha with indicator excluded)
Persuading	0.54
Contacting	0.53
Campaigning	0.53
Cooperating	0.50
Protesting	0.55
Voting	0.63

3.1   *Main independent variables*

The main independent variables used to test the hypotheses previously discussed are ideological self-placement (which we label SELF), the squared value of this term (to account for radical positions), PROXIMITY to the outgoing government's position, and *winner/loser status* with respect to the incumbent government. The first two variables are taken directly from answers to the survey question that asks respondents to position themselves on a 0–10 left-right scale.[6] For the third item, the position of each government is calculated using citizen placements of political parties (or presidential candidates) on the same left-right scale.[7] To identify the parties belonging to the outgoing cabinet, we consider the temporally closest cabinet preceding the survey date. As respondents report their level of participation at the time when the surveys are conducted (second column in Table 2.1), the theoretically relevant government is the one in power during the period leading up to these elections.[8] For example, in the case of Italy 2006, ideological proximity and winner/loser status are measured against the Berlusconi cabinet, which was the incumbent going into the 2006 general election.[9] Then we apply the formula discussed in Chapter 1 to estimate PROXIMITY. Finally, winner/loser status derives from respondents' recall of how they voted in the previous election, with those who did not vote for one of the incumbent governing parties coded as 1, and the remainder coded as 0. We therefore label this variable $LOSER_{t-1}$.

Figure 2.1 reports the distribution of the variable PROXIMITY for electoral winners and losers. As one would expect, both panels shown a notable difference between the two groups, with electoral winners on average having a lower value of PROXIMITY than losers (−1.99 and −2.58, respectively; the difference is statistically significant at the .000 level). However, the box-blots (right panel of Figure 2.1) suggest considerable variance within both groups with respect to PROXIMITY, and highlight a point that we noted earlier: that is, ideological proximity and being an electoral winner are not equivalent. This has an important consequence on the relationship between proximity, winner/loser status and

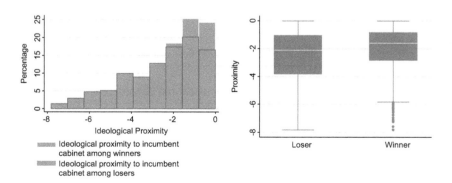

Figure 2.1 Citizen–government PROXIMITY by winner/loser status: overall distribution (left panel) and box-plots (right panel)

incentives to participate, pointing indirectly at the relevance of the winner/loser status conditional hypothesis previously proposed.

3.2 Control variables

We control for several individual level characteristics. In addition to the standard demographic controls (age, gender, education, as well as age squared to take into account a possible non-linear relationship between age and political actions), one would expect that how citizens perceive their government's competence affects their likelihood of their interest articulation. Therefore, our equations take into consideration respondents' views on (a) whether democracy is a better system of governance, and (b) assessment of government performance (see Box 2.2). We also control for other micro-level variables identified in the literature as important influences on citizens' proclivity for participation, such as income and attendance of religious services (see previous discussion).

There are also several country-level variables that scholars have identified as potentially relevant. First, we distinguish between new and established democracies, with the latter defined as countries that have experienced at least 25 years of uninterrupted democratic rule (Svolik 2008). For example, Spain and Portugal, which transitioned from authoritarian rule in the mid-1970s, are considered established democracies by the turn of the century, whereas Eastern European and Latin American cases in the 'Third Wave' are coded as new democracies. One can expect higher levels of participation in established democracies where most citizens grew up in an environment in which voluntary political action is the norm.

Box 2.2   Survey question wording for government performance and democratic evaluation variables

Assessment of government performance

*   Now thinking about the performance of the government in [Country] in general, how good or bad a job do you think the government/president has done over the past [number of years between the previous and the present election OR change in government] years. Has it/he/she done a very good job? A good job? A bad job? A very bad job?

Assessment of democratic system

*   Please tell me how strongly you agree or disagree with the following statement: 'Democracy may have problems but it's better than any other form of government.' (Do you agree strongly, agree, disagree or disagree strongly with this statement?)

Next, we consider the quality of formal political institutions. We take institutions to broadly mean 'rules of the game in a society' (see Wagner et al. 2009). This variable is operationalized by the first dimension scores extracted from a principal component analysis of the widely used World Bank governance indicators relating to effectiveness, regulatory efficiency, the rule of law, lack of corruption, voice and accountability, and political stability (Kaufmann et al. 2002).[10] Assuming that good governance is enhanced when institutions work well, one may expect that the higher the institutional quality in a given country, the less need citizens would feel to devote extra time and effort into various activities to redress an unsatisfactory status quo. In other words, insofar as high institutional quality makes a difference to participation, the relationship would likely be negative. Once again, however, this may be less applicable to voting than other activities.

Macro-level economic factors can also play an important role, with citizens in poorer countries having greater incentive to seek changes to the status quo. Even in relatively wealthy countries, economic downturns can arouse discontent leading to engagement in political activities beyond voting. In view of this, we include countries' average growth rate in the five years preceding each survey, and expect a negative relationship between change in gross domestic product (GDP) and participation.[11]

Given that some studies found a relationship between political participation (van der Meer et al. 2009) and the existence of an institutional framework that favours a consensual style of decision-making, we include a variable that captures the strength of institutional checks and balances (and therefore the diffusion of power; see Keefer 2007[12]) in each country, as well as the Gallagher index of disproportionality to account for the impact of electoral rules (see also our previous discussion on electoral rules).[13] Both variables serve as proxies reflecting the difference between consensual and majoritarian systems (Aarts and Thomassen 2008; Lijphart 1999).

To control for the possible impact of different party system formats across time and countries, we also include a measure of party system polarization. This variable is calculated using the index proposed by Dalton (2008) that corresponds mathematically to the weighted population standard deviation of party positions in a given election. The consequences of polarization on political participation and voting can be complex. For example, citizens holding radical views are more likely to find at least one party close to their views in a polarized system, and therefore more likely to turn out. Similarly, one can speculate that radicals who would otherwise resort to extra-parliamentary means may instead be channelled toward the voting booth in a highly polarized system, reducing the former forms of political participation.

Finally, we include a variable for compulsory voting. If voting is legally required, the state in effect forcibly raises turnout (Engelen 2007; Jackman 1987). Following experts' assessments in the CSES dataset, we classify compulsory voting into three categories: strongly enforced, partially enforced and non-compulsory. Note that Compulsory Voting is used only in the models employed to explain the voting variable.[14] Table 2.3 summarizes all the variables used in our analysis.

Table 2.3 Independent variables and coding

	Coding description
Individual-Level Attributes	
PROXIMITY	Ideological proximity to incumbent cabinet
LOSER$_{t-1}$	Dummy: 1 if loser in previous election
SELF	Left-to-right ideological placement on 0–10 scale
SELF squared	
Democracy better	Dummy variable: if 1, a citizen thinks democracy is better than any other form of government
Sex	Dummy variable (0 = female, 1 = male)
Age	Actual age
Age squared	Squared values of actual age
Education	1 = lowest; 8 = highest
Government performance	1 = government doing a very good job; 4 = government doing a very bad job
Income	1 = lowest household income quintile; 5 = highest household income quintile
Religious attendance	1 = never attend; 6 = most frequent attendance
Country-Year Attributes	
New democracies	0 if democracy has been in place for over 25 years; 1 otherwise
Quality of institutions	First factor of PCA on the World Bank indices of quality of government
Average GDP growth	Country's average growth rate in the five years preceding each survey
Gallagher index	Proxy for non-proportionality in electoral system
Checks and balances	1 = no checks and balances; 7 = strongest checks and balances
Ideological polarization	Ideological polarization of the party system (Dalton Index 2008)
Compulsory voting	0 = non-compulsory; 1 = compulsory, partially enforced; 2 = compulsory, strongly enforced

Unfortunately not all these pieces of information are available in all surveys. Specifically, income was not asked in Belgium, while the question on church attendance is not included in Canada, Finland, Norway, Spain, Chile, Peru and Taiwan (2004). We have therefore adopted the following strategy: we first ran the analyses by employing those independent variables that maximize the number of higher-level cases (i.e. of electoral surveys), followed by several robustness checks by including the remaining control variables.

4. Empirical findings (1): explaining political participation

Before proceeding with our analysis, it is important to recognize that our dataset is hierarchically organized, with one level (respondents) embedded within another (country[15]). Ignoring this multilevel character of the data could affect the validity of our estimation, since this could lead to residuals that are not independent within the same country, violating one crucial assumption of all statistical models (Raudenbush and Byrk 2002; Steenbergen and Jones 2002). To deal with these methodological concerns, we used a multilevel model that allows for each observation to be correlated within countries. This is achieved by including a random intercepts at the country level in the analysis to capture country differences in the propensity of respondents to engage in political actions that are not picked up by the systematic (fixed) variables in the model. We believe this is the most appropriate method to take both individual and country effects into account.[16] More formally, the equation that we have estimated is as follows:

$$y_{ij} = \alpha + \beta \mathbf{X}_{ij} + \delta \mathbf{Z}_j + \zeta_j + \varepsilon_{ij} \tag{2.1}$$

where y_{ij} is the value that respondent i living in country j has for the index of political participation; $\mathbf{X}_{ij}$ are vectors of individual-level explanatory variables; $\mathbf{Z}_j$ are vectors of country explanatory variables; and β and δ describe the salience of the previous two vectors, respectively, in the respondent's choice. $\zeta_j + \varepsilon_{ij}$ is the error term. More precisely, ζ_j is the country error term; it differs between countries but has a constant value for any given country; ε_{ij} is the error term unique for each respondent i living in country j that is assumed to be uncorrelated with $\mathbf{X}_{ij}$, $\mathbf{Z}_j$ and ζ_j.

What role do ideological and electoral considerations play in explaining political participation? Table 2.4 reports the models we have estimated to answer this question.[17] The first, atheoretical model (so-called Null Model; see Rabe-Hesketh and Skrondal 2008), does not include Level 1 or Level 2 predictors, and thus allows us to decompose the total variance in our dependent variable between the individual and country levels. Through this we can estimate the so-called intra-class correlation, ρ, a measure that tells us how much of the total variation in the political participation index can be explained solely by differences between country-election surveys. Formally: $\rho = \text{Var}(\zeta_j)/\text{Var}(\zeta_j + \varepsilon_{ij})$, where $\text{Var}(\varepsilon_{ij})$ is the variance component of the index of participation at the individual level and $\text{Var}(\zeta_j)$ is the variance component at the country level. Therefore, approximately 11 per cent of the difference in the index of participation can be explained simply by the fact that respondents come from different countries.[18] Moreover, the variance at Level 2 is significant at the 99 per cent level, while the likelihood ratio test that controls if the variance at Level 2 (i.e. country-election level) is equal to 0 can be safely rejected at standard significance levels.[19] These results confirm the appropriateness of using multilevel analysis. Note that this also holds true for all the models estimated in the subsequent chapters.

Model 1 allows us to empirically control for Hypotheses 1 to 3. Results show that both hypotheses pertaining to individual ideological self-placements seem to find empirical corroboration. This is illustrated in Figure 2.2. In the left panel, we plotted the expected value of the index of participation as the value of SELF

	Null Model	Model 1	Model 2	Model 3	Model 4	Mode 4B
Individual-Level Attributes						
PROXIMITY		−0.020**	−0.013*	0.013	−0.008	0.011
		(0.006)	(0.006)	(0.008)	(0.015)	(0.019)
LOSER$_{t-1}$			0.071***	−0.026	−0.013	0.012
			(0.015)	(0.025)	(0.047)	(0.061)
PROXIMITY* LOSER$_{t-1}$				−0.044***	−0.066***	−0.064**
				(0.009)	(0.017)	(0.021)
SELF		−0.181***	−0.191***	−0.191***	−0.223***	−0.270***
		(0.014)	(0.014)	(0.014)	(0.026)	(0.032)
SELF squared		0.015***	0.016***	0.016***	0.020***	0.024***
		(0.001)	(0.001)	(0.001)	(0.002)	(0.003)
Democracy better		0.080**	0.081**	0.079**	0.175***	0.115+
		(0.025)	(0.025)	(0.025)	(0.048)	(0.062)
Gender		0.146***	0.146***	0.145***	0.284***	0.323***
		(0.014)	(0.014)	(0.014)	(0.026)	(0.034)
Age		0.026***	0.026***	0.026***	0.039***	0.039***
		(0.003)	(0.003)	(0.003)	(0.005)	(0.007)
Age squared		−0.000***	−0.000***	−0.000***	−0.000***	−0.000***
		(0.000)	(0.000)	(0.000)	(0.000)	(0.000)
Education		0.093***	0.093***	0.092***	0.136***	0.127***
		(0.004)	(0.004)	(0.004)	(0.008)	(0.011)
Government performance		0.041***	0.030*	0.028**	0.028	0.045+
		(0.010)	(0.010)	(0.010)	(0.020)	(0.026)
Income						0.042**
						(0.014)
Church attendance						0.090***
						(0.011)

(*Continued*)

Table 2.4 Continued

	Null Model	Model 1	Model 2	Model 3	Model 4	Mode 4B
Country-Level Attributes						
New democracies		−0.203	−0.213	−0.214	−0.455	−0.691
		(0.174)	(0.174)	(0.175)	(0.419)	(0.527)
Quality of institutions		0.012	0.011	0.010	0.050	0.043
		(0.038)	(0.038)	(0.038)	(0.091)	(0.117)
Average GDP growth		0.002	0.000	0.002	−0.013	−0.045
		(0.040)	(0.040)	(0.040)	(0.096)	(0.109)
Gallagher index		0.004	0.003	0.003	−0.004	−0.024
		(0.013)	(0.013)	(0.013)	(0.032)	(0.036)
Checks and balances		0.018	0.018	0.014	0.070	0.073
		(0.056)	(0.056)	(0.056)	(0.135)	(0.161)
Party-system polarization		−0.117*	−0.117*	−0.120*	−0.267*	−0.206
		(0.052)	(0.052)	(0.052)	(0.125)	(0.163)
Constant	0.916***	0.311	0.425	0.413	−0.757	−0.901
	(0.069)	(0.337)	(0.338)	(0.339)	(0.803)	(0.943)
St. Deviation at Level 2	0.408***	0.343***	0.344***	0.345***	0.827^{***}	0.890^{***}
St. Deviation at Level 1	1.148***	1.121***	1.121***	1.120***	$\sqrt{\pi^2/3}$	$\sqrt{\pi^2/3}$
Rho	0.112	0.086	0.086	0.086	0.172	0.194
Likelihood-ratio test variance at Level 2 = 0	1972.26***	1435.97***	1430.85***	1414.03***	1903.72***	1220.3***
N (Level 1)	27,172	27,172	27,172	27,172	27,172	16,856
N (Level 2)	35	35	35	35	35	27
AIC	84763.47	83505.12	83486.12	83462.44	34027.28	20944.30
Log likelihood	−42378.73	−41734.56	−41724.06	−41711.22	−16994.64	−10451.15

Standard errors in parentheses; + $p < 0.10$, * $p < 0.05$, ** $p < 0.01$, *** $p < 0.001$

Note: Null Model and Models 1 to 3: Random-Effects Maximum Likelihood Regression;

Models 4 and 4B: Random-Effects Maximum Likelihood Logit

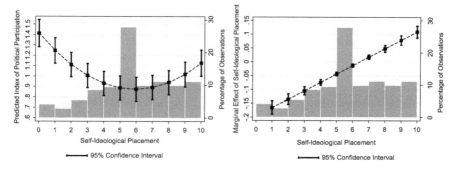

Figure 2.2 The impact of SELF on the expected value of the index of participation (left panel) and its marginal effect (right panel)

Note: The reported expected values and their corresponding confidence intervals are calculated via simulation using 10,000 draws from the estimated coefficient vector and variance–covariance matrix using the estimations of Model 1.

changes, holding all other variables fixed at their mean. A histogram depicting the frequency distribution of SELF is superimposed (the scale is shown on the vertical axis on the right-hand side of Figure 2.2). One can easily see that Model 1 suggests a quadratic relationship. While conservatives indeed participate less than progressives, as predicted by our *ideological orientation* hypothesis, it is also apparent that groups at both extremes participate more than centrists, as predicted by the *ideological extremism* hypothesis. As one moves from left to right, the index of participation decreases until it reaches a minimum between five and six, that is, around the mid-point of the ideological scale, after which it increases again. In short, citizens professing radical views (whether leftist or rightist) tend to participate more.

The right panel of Figure 2.2 tells the same story by focusing on the marginal impact on the index of participation as ideological self-placement changes. Moving SELF from 0 to 1 (that is, becoming slightly less radical) decreases the index of participation by .165 (−21 per cent in relative terms). Albeit at a rapidly decaying rate, increasing ideological self-placement by 1 unit up to 6 always decreases individuals' likelihood of political participation. However, after passing the middle of the left-right scale, increasing self-placement by 1 unit has the effect of boosting participation. For example, moving from 9 to 10 (i.e. toward a more radical position) increases the expected value of the index of participation by 0.109 (+14 per cent in relative terms).

The *ideological proximity* hypothesis also finds empirical support: the PROXIMITY variable is significant and has a negative sign as we expected. Regarding its substantive impact, according to Model 1, if PROXIMITY increases from its first to its third quartile (i.e. from −3.2 to −0.9), the index of participation would decrease by around 6 per cent.[20] Note that citizens who place themselves toward the extremes of the left-right scale are generally more distant from their government's position, which is not surprising since there have been very few ideologically radical governments. That said, the fact that PROXIMITY remains significant after controlling for ideological extremism through the inclusion of the squared term of SELF in the model clearly implies that hypotheses 2 and 3 are both valid in explaining political participation. Van der Meer et al. (2009) connected the two hypotheses to different mechanisms: the *ideological extremism* hypothesis can be better understood by relying on the equity–fairness theory (political participation is mainly motivated by relative deprivation, that is, a perceived gap between expectations and outcomes), while the *ideological proximity* hypothesis can be accounted for by the general incentives theory (citizens are chiefly motivated by beneficial outcomes and the process of participation).

Moving to Model 2, we can see that Hypothesis 4 is confirmed: the variable $LOSER_{t-1}$ is significant and positive, implying that citizens who are electoral winners subsequently participate less than losers, and the index of participation for losers is 8.8 per cent higher than that for winners. Including the winner/loser status variable in Model 2 does not change our previous results, as the PROXIMITY variable remains statistically significant. This implies that PROXIMITY and $LOSER_{t-1}$ exert independent effects on the dependent variable. But this is not the last word on the issue. In fact, Hypothesis 5 (*winner/loser status conditional hypothesis*) suggests an impact of $LOSER_{t-1}$ on political participation that is conditional on the level of PROXIMITY. To test this final hypothesis, we add an interaction term between PROXIMITY and $LOSER_{t-1}$ in Model 3. This interaction term turns out to be highly significant, and the overall empirical fit of the model is improved, as seen by the lower value of the Akaike information criterion (AIC).

It follows that our interpretation of the impact of PROXIMITY and $LOSER_{t-1}$ on political participation need to be revised, given that the marginal impact of either variable will be affected by the value assumed by its respective mediating variable. The upper panel of Figure 2.3 shows the marginal impact on the index of participation of $LOSER_{t-1}$ as the value of PROXIMITY changes. Being a past loser makes you more inclined to participate when the government you did not vote for adopts policy positions far from your own preferences. The impact is quite marked: if you are a loser and the government is around −5 in terms of PROXIMITY, the index of participation increases by a substantial 24 per cent. In other words, being a loser increases subsequent participation unless the government occupies an ideological position that comes close to your own preferences (i.e. a value of PROXIMITY equal or larger than −1: around 23 per cent of the respondents coded as losers satisfy this condition), in which case your views would likely have been reflected in the incumbent government's policies.

The lower panel of Figure 2.3 tells a complementary story: the marginal impact of increasing PROXIMITY from its first to its third quartile on the index of participation as $LOSER_{t-1}$ changes (i.e. from being a winner to a loser). As the figure reveals, the ideological proximity effect, that is, citizen' becoming less prone to participate when they are close to the incumbent government's position and hence likely to have benefited from its policies, applies *only* to past losers. For losers, if PROXIMITY increases from its first to its third quartile, the index of participation

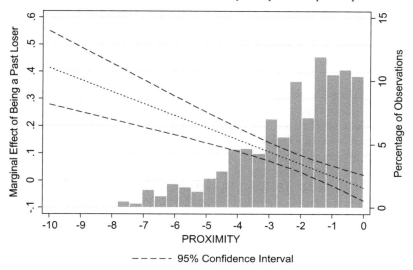

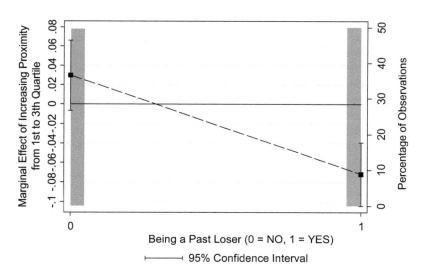

Figure 2.3 The marginal effect on the index of participation of Loser $_{t-1}$ as PROXIMITY changes (upper panel) and of PROXIMITY as Loser $_{t-1}$ changes (lower panel)

Note: The reported expected values and their corresponding confidence intervals are calculated via simulation using 10,000 draws from the estimated coefficient vector and variance–covariance matrix using the estimations of Model 3.

would decrease by 9 per cent.[21] In contrast, PROXIMITY does not reach a conventional level of significance for winners, even though the coefficient has a positive sign (implying with that winners would participate more as their distance from the incumbent cabinet shrinks). One can speculate that while winners are relatively satisfied with the fact that they helped to elect the government, losers pay more attention to what that government actually does (or does not do). In sum, the two panels show that PROXIMITY has both a (substantial) direct and an indirect impact (mediated by LOSER$_{t-1}$) on political participation. We will return to this point later.

As noted earlier, in our sample citizens did not seem to invest much time and effort on political participation; the large majority of respondents either did not participate at all (0 on our index of participation; 56 per cent of the sample), or just took part in one type of activity (23 per cent of the sample). As a robustness check, we therefore changed our index of participation into a dummy, 1 for anyone who took part in at least one type of activity, and 0 otherwise; this new dependent variable is labelled POLITICAL PARTICIPATION DUMMY. Given the nature of our dependent variable, we have estimated a random-effects maximum likelihood logit, with the following equation:

$$\text{logit}\left\{\Pr(y_{ij} \neq 0 | \mathbf{X}_{ij}, \mathbf{Z}_j)\right\} = \alpha + \beta \mathbf{X}_{ij} + \delta \mathbf{Z}_j + \zeta_j + \varepsilon_{ij} \tag{2.2}$$

where $\Pr(y_{ij} \neq 0 | \mathbf{X}_{ij}, \mathbf{Z}_j)$ is the probability that respondent i living in country j participates in at least one type of political action given the set of independent variables we are including in our model.[22] The random-effects maximum likelihood logit has been estimated through an ordinary quadrature approximation to ensure accurate estimates. As shown in Model 4, our results remain quite stable under this different model specification. For example, being an electoral loser increases the likelihood to participate (by 8 per cent if you are a loser and the government is around −5 in terms of PROXIMITY); on the other hand, moving from the first to the third quartile of PROXIMITY decreases the probability to participate in any form by 4.2 per cent among electoral losers, while once again having no significant impact on winners.

As a final robustness check, in Model 4B we replicate Model 4 by controlling for two variables often deemed relevant in the political participation literature: income and religious attendance. Adding these two control variables does not affect our main findings despite the fact that the sample size is smaller compared with Model 4 (27 rather than 35 country–elections). As can be seen, however, all our previous results hold intact even under Model 4B.

With respect to the control variables, all models concur that men tend to be more engaged than women, that higher education and a negative assessment of government performance encourages participation, and that there is a curvilinear relationship with regard to age: up to around age 50, citizens participate more as they become older, but after that, participation begins to drop off. As expected, the democratic evaluation variable has a positive and significant impact on participation. These results do not change when income and religious attendance are added in Model 4B. The most striking finding, however, is that none of the macro-level variables seems to affect political participation except party system polarization, which exerts a substantially negative impact as expected. Table 2.5 reports the expected impact of all control variables on the index of participation.

Table 2.5 Expected impact of the control variables on the probability of being involved in at least one mode of political participation

Control Variables	Expected Impact	95% c.i.	
Individual-Level Attributes			
Government performance[b]	+0.7%	−0.3%	+1.6%
Democracy better[a]	+4.3%	+2.0%	+6.6%
Age (at age = 20)[c]	+4.5%	+3.1%	+5.8%
Age (at age = 50)[c]	−1.7%	−2.2%	−1.2%
Gender[a]	+7.0%	+5.7%	+8.3%
Education[b]	+10.1%	+9.0%	+11.3%
Income[b]	+2.1%	+0.7%	+3.4%
Church attendance[b]	+8.9%	+6.7%	+11.0%
Country-Level Attributes			
New democracies[a]	−11.0%	−30.3%	+9.1%
Avg. growth five years[b]	−0.5%	−7.5%	+6.8%
Quality of institutions[b]	+4.4%	−11.0%	+20.4%
Party-system polarization[b]	−11.6%	−22.0%	−0.8%
Gallagher index[b]	−0.4%	−5.7%	+5.2%
Checks and balances[b]	+3.5%	−9.2%	+16.6%

Note: [a]expected impact by a unit increase; [b]expected impact of increasing the variable from first to third quartile of its sample distribution; [c]expected impact of increasing age of 10 years. The expected impacts are constructed using parameter estimates for Model 4 from Table 2.4 holding all other variables fixed at their means, with the exception of the expected impacts of *Income* and *Church attendance* that are estimated using parameter estimates for Model 4B from Table 2.4.

5. Empirical findings (2): explaining turnout

Next, we turn our attention to voting. Our dependent variable is a dummy: turning out or abstaining in the election for which the survey was conducted. Just as we did for Models 4 and 4b, we use therefore a random-effects maximum likelihood logit:

$$\text{logit}\left\{\Pr(y_{ij} \neq 0 | \mathbf{X}_{ij}, \mathbf{Z}_j)\right\} = \alpha + \beta\mathbf{X}_{ij} + \delta\mathbf{Z}_j + \zeta_j + \varepsilon_{ij} \qquad (2.3)$$

where $\Pr(y_{ij} \neq 0 | \mathbf{X}_{ij}, \mathbf{Z}_j)$ is now the probability that respondent i living in country j went to the polls given the set of independent variables included in our model.

Following the same approach as in the preceding section, empirical results largely resemble those previously shown and discussed, with two following exceptions discussed. To save space, Table 2.6 only shows the models most crucial for our explanations. Models 5 and 6 allow us test Hypotheses 1–5.

Table 2.6 The determinants of voting

	Model 5	Model 6	Model 6B
Individual-Level Attributes			
PROXIMITY	0.005	0.047$^+$	0.062$^+$
	(0.022)	(0.027)	(0.033)
LOSER$_{t-1}$	0.235***	0.065	0.104
	(0.052)	(0.082)	(0.105)
PROXIMITY* LOSER$_{t-1}$		−0.077**	−0.082*
		(0.029)	(0.036)
SELF	−0.141**	−0.143**	−0.186**
	(0.049)	(0.049)	(0.059)
SELF squared	0.014**	0.014**	0.016**
	(0.005)	(0.005)	(0.005)
Democracy better	0.332***	0.330***	0.330***
	(0.072)	(0.072)	(0.090)
Gender	0.049	0.048	0.074
	(0.046)	(0.046)	(0.059)
Age	0.096***	0.095***	0.083***
	(0.009)	(0.009)	(0.011)
Age squared	−0.001***	−0.001***	−0.001***
	(0.000)	(0.000)	(0.000)
Education	0.108***	0.108***	0.104***
	(0.015)	(0.015)	(0.020)
Government performance	−0.130***	−0.133***	−0.137**
	(0.034)	(0.034)	(0.043)
Income			0.054*
			(0.024)
Religious attendance			0.111***
			(0.020)
Country-Level Attributes			
New democracies	−0.244	−0.247	−0.506
	(0.311)	(0.311)	(0.308)
Quality of institutions	0.090	0.089	0.096
	(0.069)	(0.069)	(0.069)
Average GDP growth	−0.069	−0.067	−0.154*
	(0.071)	(0.070)	(0.064)
Gallagher index	−0.025	−0.025	−0.046*
	(0.024)	(0.024)	(0.022)
Checks and balances	−0.017	−0.025	0.137
	(0.102)	(0.102)	(0.098)
Party-system polarization	−0.094	−0.099	−0.064
	(0.095)	(0.095)	(0.096)

	Model 5	Model 6	Model 6B
Compulsory voting	0.637**	0.647**	0.386+
	(0.200)	(0.200)	(0.234)
Constant	0.670	0.649	0.398
	(0.651)	(0.649)	(0.638)
St. Deviation at Level 2	0.605***	0.603***	0.498***
St. Deviation at Level 1	$\sqrt{\pi^2/3}$	$\sqrt{\pi^2/3}$	$\sqrt{\pi^2/3}$
Rho	0.100	0.100	0.070
Likelihood–ratio test variance at Level 2 = 0	456.73***	451.46***	199.01***
N (Level 1)	29,703	29,703	18,616
N (Level 2)	36	36	28
AIC	14158.054	14153.026	8938.22
Log likelihood	−7060.027	−7056.513	−4447.11

Standard errors in parentheses; $^+ p < 0.10$, $^* p < 0.05$, $^{**} p < 0.01$, $^{***} p < 0.001$

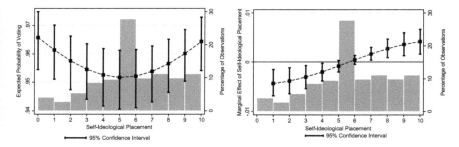

Figure 2.4 The impact of SELF on the expected probability of turnout (left panel) and its marginal effect (right panel)

Note: The reported expected values and their corresponding confidence intervals are calculated via simulation using 10,000 draws from the estimated coefficient vector and variance–covariance matrix using the estimations of Model 5.

Let's start with the impact of SELF on voting. Figure 2.4 reveals that only the *ideological extremism* hypothesis is supported, albeit to a less extent compared with what we found for the index of political participation. Respondents self-placed toward both ends of the left-right spectrum are more likely to vote than those around the centre. We should add that although this difference is statistically significant, the substantial impact is negligible, as the right panel of Figure 2.4 shows. For example, moving SELF from 0 to 1 or from 9 to 10 on the left-right scale, while holding all other variables fixed at their means, decreases the probability of turnout by less than 0.5 per cent.

Hypothesis 4 also finds empirical corroboration in explaining turnout. Electoral losers are 1.2 per cent more likely to vote than winners (a difference significant at the 95 per cent confidence interval). On the contrary – and this is the second notable difference from results reported for other modes of political participation –

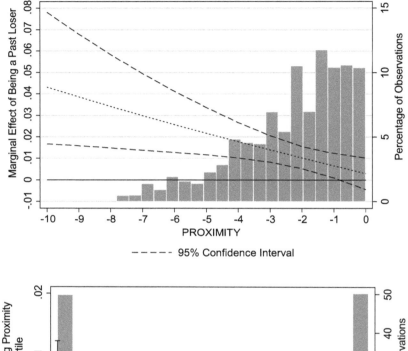

Figure 2.5 The marginal effect on the probability of turnout of Loser $_{t-1}$ as PROXIMITY changes (upper panel) and of PROXIMITY as Loser $_{t-1}$ changes (lower panel)

Note: The reported expected values and their corresponding confidence intervals are calculated via simulation using 10,000 draws from the estimated coefficient vector and variance–covariance matrix using the estimations of Model 6.

citizen–government ideological proximity does not have any direct impact on voting. This result is in line with those reported in previous studies such as van der Meer et al. (2009).

However, this does not imply that ideological proximity has no impact on voting. When an interaction term between LOSER$_{t-1}$ and PROXIMITY is introduced in Model 6, it turns out to be highly significant for turnout, just as in the previous section. This result helps us better grasp the complex effects of ideological factors on voting. Moreover, adding this interaction term once again improves the model, as evidenced by a lower value of the Akaike information criterion in Model 6 compared to Model 5. The marginal impact of LOSER$_{t-1}$ changes substantively according to ideological proximity (see Figure 2.5). Being a loser makes you more likely to vote only when your own position is very far away from that of the incumbent government. This suggests that the act of voting is in part motivated by a desire for change, so that citizens who are content with the incumbent government's policies have less incentive to go to the polls. Note the magnitude of this effect: if you are a loser with the value of PROXIMITY to the incumbent government around −5, your likelihood of turning out increases by 2.2 per cent.

Model 6B runs a robustness check on the results found in Model 6 by adding the income and religious church attendance variables. These additions do not affect our main conclusions.

Concerning the control variables, explanations for turnout are quite similar to those that account for other modes of political participation. In general, higher education and more positive assessments of democracy encourage voting, though gender has no significant impact. Interestingly, turnout increases with affirmative opinions on government performance, which is the opposite of what we found for other political activities. Once again, there is a curvilinear relationship with respect to age, with the oldest and youngest cohorts least likely to vote. Note that turnout reaches a peak at around 63, an age markedly older than what we found for other political activities. As for the macro-level variables, not surprisingly, there is a strong tendency to vote in countries where turnout is compulsory, while, at least in Model 6B, the likelihood of voting decreases when the economy is doing well and when the Gallagher index increases (that is, when the electoral rules produce disproportional outcomes, a result that contradicts some previous findings). This last finding is however coherent with Policzer (2000:838), who found no evidence that consensual democracies are more egalitarian and representative of citizens' opinions and argued instead that 'regarding citizens' participation in politics, majoritarianism outperforms consensualism' because under the former, political participation is more common without being more unequal. Keep in mind, however, that the sample in Model 6B is smaller compared to the other models. Table 2.7 reports the expected impact of all control variables on the probability of turnout.

Conclusion

In this chapter, we have shown how ideological factors can influence whether citizens engage in different modes of political action. Specifically, citizens with

Table 2.7 Expected impact of the control variables on the probability of voting

Control Variables	Expected Impact	95% c.i.	
Individual-Level Attributes			
Government performance[b]	−0.6%	−1.0%	−0.3%
Democracy better[a]	+1.8%	+0.9%	+2.7%
Age (at age = 20)[c]	+6.0%	+4.4%	+7.6%
Age (at age = 50)[c]	+0.5%	+0.3%	+0.7%
Gender[a]	+0.2%	−0.2%	+0.7%
Education[b]	+1.5%	+1.0%	+2.0%
Income[b]	+0.6%	+0.1%	+1.1%
Church attendance[b]	+2.3%	+1.4%	+3.3%
Country-Level Attributes			
New democracies[a]	−1.3%	−4.6%	+1.6%
Avg. growth five years[b]	−0.5%	−1.6%	+0.6%
Quality of institutions[b]	+1.3%	−0.8%	+3.4%
Party-system polarization[b]	−0.7%	−2.1%	+0.7%
Gallagher index[b]	−0.4%	−1.1%	+0.4%
Checks and balances[b]	−0.2%	−2.1%	+1.7%
Compulsory voting[b]	+2.7%	+1.2%	+4.3%

Note: [a]expected impact by a unit increase; [b]expected impact of increasing the variable from first to third quartile of its sample distribution; [c]expected impact of increasing age of 10 years. The expected impacts are constructed using parameter estimates for Model 6 from Table 2.6 holding all other variables fixed at their means, with the exception of the expected impacts of *Income* and *Church attendance* that are estimated using parameter estimates for Model 6B from Table 2.6.

radical views (especially on the left) are more inclined than moderates to contact politicians or government officials, work in election campaigns and join protests (see Figure 2.2). The same holds true with regard to election turnout, albeit with a smaller difference between radicals and moderates (Figure 2.4). We also find that ideological proximity between citizens and their (incumbent) government indeed plays an important role in explaining political participation, and that this effect is exerted not only directly, but also indirectly through the mediating impact of electoral winner/loser status. This is clearly illustrated in Figures 2.3 and 2.5. Once again, while significant in both cases, the impact of this factor is more limited for voting than for other activities. Compared with the latter, turnout requires fewer resources (time, effort, etc.), so that for most people casting a ballot is much easier than, say, persuading a neighbour to support a certain party or candidate, writing a letter or e-mail to a representative regarding issues one is concerned about, or taking part in a demonstration. We believe that the greater the commitment required for a given activity, the more important the role of ideological self-placement and distance from the government would be.

Moreover, the impact of ideological proximity should be considered jointly with one's vote choice in the last election. If you voted for a party or candidate that did not enter government – that is, if you are an electoral 'loser' – but the government ends up pursuing policies that closely reflect your preferences, then your likelihood of turning out or participating in other political activities would remain unchanged. In contrast, if this government implements or promises measures that are contrary to what you would like to see, then you would be more inclined to vote or engage in other forms of political participation.

It is worthwhile expounding on some implication of our findings. According to what we noted in Chapter 1 (see Figure 1.6 and 1.7), an ideologically moderate government tends to minimize the distance between itself and a large majority of citizens who place themselves around the middle of the left-right spectrum. The findings discussed in this chapter show that such a government *reduces* the incentive to participate among electoral losers (left panels of Figures 2.3 and 2.5). Conversely, an ideologically radical government tends to maximize citizen–government distance for a large majority of the population. Therefore, it would increase participation, at least among electoral losers who would have greater incentive to become active in order to articulate demands to an ideologically distant government.

In view of this, in terms of boosting political participation (especially once we consider costly forms of such participation), ideologically radical governments outperform moderate ones. But before one (mis)takes this conclusion as an endorsement of extremist parties or candidates, we should pause and ponder about the potential ramifications of encouraging everyone to become political active as often as possible. In a pioneering work that established the empirical study of political culture, Almond and Verba (1963) classified citizen orientations into three categories – parochial, subject and participant – and stated that an ideal 'civic culture' is not achieved by raising the proportion of citizens with a participatory orientation to the highest possible extent; in fact, having too many active participants may impose an excessively heavy burden on a government's ability to cope and respond. If political participation is chiefly motivated by a desire to alter the status quo, then a modest level of political engagement can suggest that citizens are relatively content with the extant system. Whether and how citizens' ideological positions and distance vis-à-vis their government affect attitudes toward the political system, that is, their level of satisfaction with how the democracy works, is the topic of our next chapter.

Notes

1 That said, a situation where nobody votes cannot be in Nash equilibrium. Indeed, if no one else votes, then you should always vote because you can decide the outcome. Similarly, neither can a situation where everyone votes be in equilibrium: if everyone else votes, then your vote is almost certain to be irrelevant to the outcome. Thus you should abstain because the costs of voting exceed any expected benefit from affecting the outcome (Morrow 1994). Palfrey and Rosenthal (1985) show that we can reach equilibrium with a turnout greater than 0 but considerably lower than 50 per cent. In this equilibrium, one's expectations of whether others will vote are equal to the marginal effect of one's own vote on the outcome. See also Goeree and Holt (2005) for laboratory experiments on strategic voter participation.

2 Data and documentation are available at www.cses.org. All the surveys considered are post-election studies.

3 Two studies of the 2002 German Bundestag elections have been included in the CSES dataset; we will only use the telephone survey. For Portugal and Taiwan, two elections each are included in the dataset, and we will use both since elections (rather than countries) are the primary unit of analysis in the CSES framework.

4 To be more precise, we ran a Polychoric Principal Component Analysis given that a Principal Component Analysis is not advisable when the variables under investigation are not continuous, as is in our case (Kolenikov and Angeles 2004).

5 In the following analyses, we use the additive scale of political participation to ease interpretation of our findings. Using the first composite score of the five participation items resulting from the principal component analysis as our dependent variable yields substantively identical results to those reported.

6 The Japanese survey used the terms *progressive* and *conservative* instead of left and right, respectively.

7 As discussed in Chapter 1, in the case of presidential and semi-presidential systems, whenever the left-right score for the winning presidential candidate is unavailable in the surveys, we use the score for this candidate's party. This information is not available for the CSES survey in Belgium, so we use party positions taken from Benoit and Laver (2006).

8 We do not count caretaker governments.

9 The data used to identify governing parties are taken from the *Database of Political Institutions 2012 (updated Jan. 2013)*. See Beck et al. (2001).

10 The six governance indicators load highly on one single factor (eigenvalue 5.75, explaining 82 per cent of total variance; the eigenvalue of the second factor is a mere 0.452).

11 Replacing this variable with GDP per capita in the year preceding the elections, as done for example in van der Meer et al. 2009, does not change any of our conclusions.

12 Higher values denote greater checks and balance. In presidential systems, CHECKS and BALANCES increases by 1 for each legislative chamber unless the president's party has a majority in the lower house. In parliamentary systems, CHECKS and BALANCES increases by 1 for every party in a coalition government that is needed to maintain a legislative majority. See Keefer and Stasavage (2003) for a completed list of conditions.

13 For presidential and semi-presidential systems, we estimate the Gallagher index using the method proposed by Lijphart (1999), that is, by taking the geometric mean of the Gallagher index for presidential and legislative elections. Replacing the Gallagher index with the mean district magnitude as a proxy of the degree of proportionality of an electoral system does not produce any notable differences in our results.

14 Including the Compulsory Voting variable in models used to explain other modes of participation does not affect any of our results; this variable always turns out to be statistically insignificant.

15 More specifically, this refers to 'country-election', given that in two cases (Taiwan and Portugal), we have two surveys for the same country in our dataset (see Note 3).

16 Replicating our analysis by employing a set of country-fixed effects does not alter any of our conclusions.

17 Portugal 2005 is not included in Table 2.4 since *campaign activity* (one of the five activities comprising our index of participation) was not asked in that survey. Also, our

analysis only includes respondents who meet voting age requirements in each country at the time of the previous election.

18 Knowing that $\text{Var}(\varepsilon_{ij})$ shown in the seventh to last row in the table is 1.32 (i.e. 1.148^2), and that the value of $\text{Var}(\zeta_j)$ shown in the eight to last row is 0.166 (i.e. 0.408^2), we can infer that the country variance in our data constitutes around the 11 per cent of the total variance (0.166/(0.166+1.32)).

19 The null hypothesis tested by a likelihood ratio test is equivalent to the hypothesis that there is no random intercept in the model. According to Table 2.4, we can reject such null hypothesis, implying that we cannot use a pooled model and instead need a random-effects model to obtain reliable statistical estimates.

20 Specifically, increasing proximity from −3.2 to −0.9 decreases the index of participation by −0.05 (a change statistically significant at the 99 per cent level). Given that the average value of the index of participation is equal to 0.801, this change corresponds to a relative decrease of 6 per cent.

21 For electoral losers, increasing PROXIMITY from −3.2 to −0.9 decreases the index of participation by 0.071 in absolute terms (statistically significant at the 99 per cent level).

22 Note that ε_{ij} in (2.2) are identically and independently logistic distributed with a mean of zero and variance $\pi^2/3$, independently of ζ_j.

3 Ideological proximity and support for democracy

Introduction

As a mechanism ensuring accountability of the governors to the governed, free elections constitute one of the defining features of democracy. Election results shape government composition and policy outputs, most likely to the advantage of voters who support the winning parties. Previous studies have addressed the gap between electoral winners and losers on political activism (as discussed in the preceding chapter), and on various dimensions of political support, from specific institutional evaluations to more diffuse aspects concerning democratic principles and procedures (Anderson and Tverdova 2001; Anderson et al. 2005; Moehler 2009). Not surprisingly, these studies reported that winners express significantly greater support than losers at each level. However, these works defined winners and losers in a static fashion by examining their attitudes at only a single point in time, and used a dichotomous categorization that does not capture possible variations within each group. This chapter considers the impact of both citizen–government ideological proximity, and the past history of winning or losing, on a commonly used indicator of political support, namely satisfaction with democracy.

Since winners stand behind parties or candidates currently holding the reins of power, it is intuitively understandable that they express greater confidence in political authorities and institutions. As a corollary, one expects their satisfaction to decline if his or her preferred parties lose power. However, in a democracy, winners have no stronger claim as 'owners' of the political system than losers, since by definition, free elections permit the fortunes of both current winning and losing parties to fluctuate at the ballot box, and thus offer losers the possibility of winning in the future. It follows that a distinction exists not only between present winners and losers, but between voters who have previous (especially recent) experience of winning and those who do not. The former should express greater approval of the political system even if their parties are currently in opposition, since the system had worked to their benefit, whereas the latter have little cause for satisfaction because their parties have long been excluded from power. In short, we take a dynamic view in defining winners and losers, taking into account not only present conditions, but also experience in the recent past, and demonstrate that both current winners who had lost in the previous election and current losers who had won in the previous election are more satisfied with democracy than voters whose parties have long been out of power.

In addition to a static definition of winners and losers, most extant literature also treats both categories as homogenous, an approach that neglects possible variations within each group. Assuming policy as one of the crucial factors influencing satisfaction levels, we argue that not all winners can equally expect to see their preferred policies implemented, and some winners (even losers) may derive greater policy benefits from the government than others. We therefore expect that, for both winners and losers, levels of satisfaction depend on how closely the government's preferences align with their own. To reiterate a previously cited example, under a socialist–communist coalition government, socialist winners may see more of their aspirations turned into policy outputs than communist winners, and social democratic losers who are closer to the government in policy terms may have less cause for dissatisfaction than conservative losers. In short, this chapter goes beyond the simple dichotomous classification of winners and losers to consider the policy distance between individual voters and their government, and shows that ideological proximity exerts a significant impact on satisfaction with democracy.

1. Conceptualizing democratic support

In March 2014, *The Economist* called attention to the health of democracy ('What's gone wrong with democracy' 2014). One problem concerns some nominal democracies sliding towards autocracy, meaning that while maintaining the outward appearance of democracy through elections, they have restricted both political and civil freedoms. Also, many established democracies are affected by widespread perception of a dysfunctional political system. The advance of democracy in many non-Western regions seems to have halted or even regressed, while publics in many Western countries appear fatigued by ongoing economic and political difficulties. In short, many people have become disillusioned with the workings of a democratic political system and lost confidence in political institutions.

This is certainly not a new phenomenon. Some scholars at the end of the twentieth century asserted that, even in countries where democracy is consolidated, a crisis of legitimacy might still persist (Norris 1999). This warning has been confirmed by successive studies on the topic, pointing to a malaise in the form of citizens in democratic countries having less trust in political parties, reduced levels of political participation, and feelings of alienation towards politics (Dalton 2004).

Many hypotheses have been advanced to explain this erosion of political support. Some scholars claim that dissatisfaction results from long-term changes in social structure and political conditions (Dalton 2004). Others argue that support for democracy is affected by (economic) performance, citizens' expectation and institutional outcomes (Anderson et al. 2005; Bellucci and Memoli 2013; Criado and Herreros 2007; Lewis-Beck and Stegmaier 2000). Other researchers attribute the decline of political support to the behaviour of political elites (e.g. scandals; see Bowler and Karp 2004; Maier 2011; Memoli 2011; Thompson 2000).

However, political support is a multifaceted and complex concept (Klingemann 1999). Before launching into an empirical analysis on support for democracy, we must first clarify theoretically the specific object of support: what exactly do citizens have in mind when they make an assessment of democracy? To define the concept of democratic support, it is useful to adopt the framework proposed by Easton (1965), who distinguishes between three political objects – the political community, the regime and the authorities – in terms of diffuse and specific support. The former refers to loyalty to one's own political community, while the latter is based on the fulfilment of demands or satisfaction with outputs.

In addition to the objects of political support, Easton distinguishes between two types of orientations: diffuse and specific. This distinction is similar to that made by Almond and Verba (1963) between affective beliefs, which involve acceptance of or identification with an entity, and evaluations, which concern a judgment on the appropriateness of the object. According to Easton, diffuse support consists of a set of ingrained attitudes toward politics and can be interpreted as an indicator of the legitimacy of a political system or political institutions. In contrast, specific support refers to satisfaction with the institutional output, that is positive assessments of the results of certain measures enacted by the state. Whereas diffuse support is more stable, specific support is susceptible to fluctuation depending on the performance of political institutions and actors.

At the empirical level, diffuse and specific support are not totally independent, because the former can alleviate a decline in the latter (Gibson 1989; Tyler 1990). Diffuse support can remains relatively high even when specific support drops sharply. This 'empirical discrepancy' can be addressed through comparisons between different levels of support, since not all unfavourable expressions towards the political system have 'the same degree of seriousness' (Easton 1975).

This theoretical framework has been refined by Norris (1999) and Dalton (2004), who distinguished five levels of political support. Specifically, they take into consideration three different objects at the regime level: *regime principles* express the normative values of the political system, reflected in the belief that democracy is the best form of government (Dalton 1999); *regime performance* refers to democratic processes (Norris 1999); and finally, *regime institutions* denote confidence in political institutions. Table 3.1 summarizes the multidimensional nature of system support previously discussed.

In this chapter, we use satisfaction with democracy as an indicator at the *regime performance* level of political support. According to Norris (2006), satisfaction with democracy is indeed an indicator of 'public evaluations of how well autocratic or democratic governments work in practice', and Blais and Gélineau (2007) argued that satisfaction with democracy, especially in democratic countries, expresses 'the actual achievements of democratic process.' Although 'satisfaction with democracy' is one of the most commonly utilized indicators of political support, its interpretation has not always been clear (see Canache et al. 2001). On the one hand, some scholars claim its use is complicated (Linde and Ekman 2003) and

Table 3.1 The multidimensional nature of system support

	Level of Analysis	Affective Orientation	Instrumental Evaluation
Diffuse support	Political community	National pride National identity	Best nation to live
	Regime: principles	Democratic values	Democracy best form of government
	Regime: performance	Partecipatory norms Political rights	Evaluation of rights Satisfaction with democracy process
	Regime: institutions	Institutional expectations Support for parties Output expectations	Performance judgments Confidence in institutions Confidence in party system
Specific support	Authorities	Feelings towards political leaders	Evaluations of politicians

Source: Dalton (1999; 2004), Norris (1999).

its meaning appears somewhat ambiguous (Norris 1999). On the other hand, different indicators have been used by various authors in order to operationalize this concept (see Castillo 2006; Dalton 1999; Klingemann 1999; Kornberg and Clarke 1994; Montero and Gunther 1994). These debates notwithstanding, democratic satisfaction should be considered an expression of short-term evaluation of system outputs (Waldron-Moore 1999) and a useful measure of the discrepancy between democratic norms and actual processes (Wagner et al. 2003).

2.   Exploring the winner/loser effect (and its implications)

In the past decade, a large number of works have analysed the determinants of satisfaction with democracy, using both individual and aggregate data (Dalton 1999; Norris 1999). One factor that has received increasing attention, as already noted, is how individuals who support parties in government (winners) and those who support parties in opposition (losers) differ in support for democratic processes and outputs. Although many studies have stressed the declining role of political parties at least since the end of the 1960s, parties still appear to have the capacity to influence citizens' political views (Dennis and Owen 2001), since parties remain key players in government formation and decision-making. As both channels of political engagement beyond the ballot box and the proportion of citizens inclined toward direct participation have markedly expanded in recent years, parties may cede part of their interest articulation role, but continue to serve a crucial interest aggregation function (Dalton and Wattenberg 2000). Since parties are still largely responsible for policymaking, voters concerned with policy outcomes should have an important stake in, and feel affected by, whether their preferred parties win or lose. The previous chapter clearly illustrated that with respect to political participation.

In this sense, if citizens decide to vote for party A instead of party B, it is because they believe it can better respond to their interests, satisfy their goals and reflect their values. How well one's party performs in an election may affect attitudes toward not only specific political authorities, but also the democratic process in general. When a voter chooses a party (or a candidate) that wins the election or at least enters into a coalition government, he or she expresses greater confidence in the government, which in turn translates into higher satisfaction with democracy (Anderson and LoTempio 2002). In contrast, electoral losers are almost always less satisfied with the way democracy works than winners (Anderson and Guillory 1997; Anderson and Tverdova 2001).[1]

Losers' discontent may affect the quality, even stability, of democracy. Hence Anderson et al. (2005:7) referred to losers as 'the crucial veto players of democratic governance,' and Nadeau and Blais (1993:553) also argued that 'the viability of electoral democracy depends on its ability to secure the support of a substantial proportion of individuals who are displeased with the outcome of an election'. Moreover, there is a risk that winners may be too compliant toward the government, to the extent of being willing to overlook violations of democratic principles (Moehler 2009).

Yet the relationship between winner/loser status and satisfaction with democracy is neither immediately self-evident nor straightforward. To examine this causal linkage in more detail, we focus on two different aspects that have been largely overlooked in the literature, including citizen–government ideological proximity, the main theme of this book.

2.1   *The absolute and marginal dynamic effect of winning*

First, there can be a dynamic pattern to the winner/loser effect given that in a democracy, today's winners could be yesterday's losers, and vice versa. Scholars have rarely examined this question directly. In one of the few exceptions, Anderson and LoTempio (2002) analysed whether backing presidential and congressional winners has a cumulative effect on levels of political trust among American voters. Using data from the 1972 and 1996 US presidential and congressional elections, they found that those who voted for the presidential winner were significantly more trusting than those who did not. In contrast, voting for the congressional majority party did not affect levels of political trust. Moreover, double winners express the highest level of trust, and winners in only the presidential or congressional contest were more trusting than double losers.

However, in modelling the dynamic pattern involved in the winner/loser dichotomy, it seems more natural to compare winning in the present election with winning in the previous election. This implies that in a presidential system, we should compare the results across two consecutive presidential races,[2] while in parliamentary systems two successive legislative elections should be compared.

This dynamic can be viewed and analysed from two alternative perspectives: the *absolute* and *marginal* effects. This difference relates to how past (present) experience affects present (past) attitudes. If we assume that people prefer more to less, including in terms of views toward the political system, then we can expect that those who have experienced only losses should be the least satisfied with democracy, those who experienced only victories should be the most satisfied, and those who experience some loss and some gain across elections should fall in between. Moreover, among the last group (mixed electoral results), we expect that those who won in the most recent election (but lost in the previous one) would express greater satisfaction than those who won in the past but lost in the latest round. This makes sense if we assume that individuals discount more distant personal experiences compared to more recent ones. Let *WW* stand for someone who won both in the present and previous elections, *LL* for a two-time loser, *WL* for someone who won in the present election but lost in the previous one, and *LW* for a voter who lost in the present election but won in the past. We expect that in terms of satisfaction with democracy, we should find the following lexicographic ranking:

Hypothesis 1a: (the 'absolute' dynamic impact [ADI] of winning): WW > WL > LW > LL

However, the dynamic pattern involved in the winning-losing effect can also be analysed from a different perspective, which focuses more on its marginal rather than absolute consequences. Following the standard theory of utility (Kreps 1990), one can reasonably assume that citizens derive a decreasing marginal utility in winning (and, for similar reasons, an increasing marginal disutility in losing). Consequently, the impact of winning today should matter more for those who have not enjoyed this experience in the recent past. In contrast, for voters who have won previously, winning today should matter less. We therefore derive the following hypothesis regarding the dynamic nature of the winner–/loser effect:

Hypothesis 1b: (the 'marginal' dynamic impact [MDI] of winning): the marginal effect of winning in the current (previous) election should matter more for citizens who lost in the previous (current) election.

Note that Hypotheses 1a and 1b are not mutually exclusive. This would happen, for example, if the marginal effect of winning in the current election matters more for citizens who lost in the previous election, but the absolute impact of being a winner in the past and in the present still remains significant. We will return to this point in greater detail later.

Before proceeding, we would like to note an emerging literature which has begun re-examining the winner/loser distinction from a dynamic perspective. Anderson et al. (2005) investigate how a winner/loser gap on democratic satisfaction evolved over time in Britain, Germany and Spain, and reported three major findings. First, when a citizen's winner/loser status changes due to government alternation, his or her level of democratic satisfaction would change as well. As a result, electoral alternation leads to a substantial shift in the winner/loser gap. Second, this gap persists over time. In other words, losers' dissatisfaction with democracy reflects not just temporary disappointment but rather discontent with the current government over the entire electoral cycle. Finally, losing repeatedly gradually undermines citizens' democratic satisfaction due to the accumulation of frustration in the electoral arena. Specifically, Anderson et al. (2005:63) found that in Britain and Germany, democratic satisfaction starts to decline for those who have lost two consecutive elections. Similarly, Chang et al. (2014) showed that voters whose preferred party has not won office are significantly less supportive of democracy compared with current losers who had been winners previously, and that this is especially true in new democracies.

2.2 The proximity effect

Previous studies on the relationship between winner/loser status and satisfaction with democracy also portrayed voters' assessments of electoral results as basically a zero-sum game, that is, that those who backed winning parties or candidates will be more satisfied than losers *regardless of other conditions*. Yet we know that even parties and voters on the same side of the winner/loser dichotomy can hold different ideological positions, and this could clearly affect political satisfaction. According to the large body of literature on the spatial theory of voting (Adams et al. 2005; Downs 1957), voters are assumed to vote for the party presenting the policy program closest to their policy preference (Orit 2005). Indeed, voters are expected to derive utility from the package of policies implemented by the future government as a function of the distance between this package and their ideal points: the shorter this distance is, the higher their utility. If proximity models can explain voters' choices at the ballot box, then it is reasonable to assume that they can also make similar assessments when evaluating democratic performance. Following Henderson (2004), we expect that for voters who backed losing parties, the closer the eventual winner is to their own ideological position, the more satisfied they would feel. This is because disutility in terms of policies implemented by the government is lower, which assuages the negative impact of being a loser. The opposite should happen with winners. In sum, greater distance between voters and the winning party exacerbates the winner/loser disparity, while this gap can be minimized by ideological propinquity. This leads to our second hypothesis:

Hypothesis 2 (the policy effect [PE] of winning): winners (losers) who are closer to the ideal point of the current government will be more satisfied with the way democracy works than winners (losers) who are located farther away.

Clearly, the cabinet's position on the underlying ideological dimension of political competition matters in this regard. Indeed, as long as the distribution of voters is approximately symmetric around some central value, as is usually the case (Ezrow 2008), then a cabinet that takes a position close to this value (rather than a more radical position) can minimize the average distance between itself and the electorate as a whole irrespective of individual voters' winner/loser status. According to Hypothesis 2, this should raise the overall level of satisfaction with democracy.

3.   Data and measurement issues

Before examining the validity of our hypotheses, it is necessary to provide detailed information about the data needed for empirical analysis. To control for our hypotheses, we once again use the Comparative Studies of Electoral Systems (CSES) survey[3] already described in Chapter 2. However, in this chapter, we use both the second and third modules of CSES (2001–2006 and 2006–2011, respectively), given that the latter module also includes all the variables we would like to test are included also in the latter module. Table 3.2 reports the list of election-surveys in our dataset. Overall, we have 73 electoral-surveys (35 from CSES2 and 38 from CSES3) covering 34 countries in CSES2, 31 countries in CSES3 and 40 countries overall.[4] Geographically, our dataset covers 5 countries from Latina America (with 10 electoral surveys), 4 from East Asia (8 surveys), 10 from Central and Eastern Europe (15 surveys), and finally, 21 Western democracies (40 surveys).

The first two columns in Table 3.2 list years for the current and previous elections analysed in this chapter, while Column 3 shows the type of election (legislative or presidential). Finally, Column 4 reports if there was any major government change (or intergovernmental change)[5] following the current election.

The advantage of using CSES data is that questionnaire items once again include the necessary information needed to construct our variables. In particular, we know: (a) the parties (or presidential candidates) for which respondents voted in the current *and* previous elections; (b) respondents' self-placement on a 11-point left-right scale; (c) placements of political parties (or presidential candidates) on the same scale.

Using the information coming from (a), we can classify a citizen's winner/loser status in both the current and previous elections. A respondent is considered a current winner if he or she voted for a party in government at the time when the CSES survey was administered. In most cases, this coincides with the first post-election cabinet. A past winner is estimated in a similar way. In this case, as done in Chapter 2, we consider the parties belonging to the incumbent government in the lead up to the current elections (we did not count any caretaker cabinet).[6]

Table 3.2 List of electoral surveys included in Chapter 3

Country	Current Election	Previous Election	Type of Election	Government Change Following Current Election
Australia	2004	2001	Legislative	no major change
Australia	2007	2004	Legislative	major change
Austria	2008	2006	Legislative	major change
Belgium	2003	1999	Legislative	no major change
Brazil	2002	1998	Presidential	major change
Brazil	2006	2002	Presidential	no major change
Brazil	2010	2006	Presidential	no major change
Bulgaria	2001	1997	Legislative	major change
Canada	2004	2000	Legislative	no major change
Canada	2008	2006	Legislative	major change
Chile	2005	1999	Presidential	major change
Chile	2009	2005	Presidential	no major change
Croatia	2007	2003	Legislative	major change
Czech Republic	2002	2000	Legislative	no major change
Czech Republic	2006	2003	Legislative	major change
Czech Republic	2010	2006	Legislative	no major change
Denmark	2001	1998	Legislative	major change
Denmark	2007	2003	Legislative	no major change
Estonia	2011	2007	Legislative	no major change
Finland	2003	1999	Legislative	major change
Finland	2007	2003	Legislative	major change
Finland	2011	2007	Legislative	major change
France	2002	1995	Presidential	no major change
France	2007	2002	Presidential	no major change
Germany	2002	1998	Legislative	no major change
Germany	2005	2002	Legislative	major change
Germany	2009	2005	Legislative	no major change
Greece	2009	2007	Legislative	major change
Hungary	2002	1998	Legislative	major change
Iceland	2003	1999	Legislative	no major change
Iceland	2007	2003	Legislative	no major change
Iceland	2009	2007	Legislative	major change
Ireland	2002	1997	Legislative	no major change
Ireland	2007	2002	Legislative	no major change
Israel	2003	1999	Legislative	major change
Israel	2006	2003	Legislative	major change
Italy	2006	2001	Legislative	major change
Japan	2004*	2001	Legislative	no major change
Japan	2007*	2004	Legislative	no major change
Latvia	2010	2006	Legislative	major change
Mexico	2003	2000	Presidential	no major change

Country	Current Election	Previous Election	Type of Election	Government Change Following Current Election
Mexico	2006	2003	Presidential	no major change
Mexico	2009	2006	Presidential	no major change
Netherlands	2002	1998	Legislative	major change
Netherlands	2006	2002	Legislative	major change
Netherlands	2010	2006	Legislative	major change
New Zealand	2002	1999	Legislative	no major change
New Zealand	2008	2005	Legislative	major change
Norway	2001	1997	Legislative	no major change
Norway	2005	2001	Legislative	major change
Norway	2009	2005	Legislative	major change
Peru	2006	2001	Presidential	major change
Peru	2011	2006	Presidential	major change
Philippines	2004	2001	Presidential	major change
Poland	2001	1997	Legislative	major change
Poland	2005	2001	Legislative	major change
Poland	2007	2005	Legislative	major change
Portugal	2002	1999	Legislative	major change
Portugal	2005	2002	Legislative	no major change
Portugal	2009	2005	Legislative	no major change
Romania	2004	2000	Presidential	major change
Romania	2009	2004	Presidential	major change
Slovakia	2010	2006	Legislative	major change
Slovenia	2004	2000	Legislative	major change
Slovenia	2008	2004	Legislative	major change
South Africa	2009	2004	Presidential	no major change
South Korea	2004	2000	Presidential	major change
South Korea	2008	2004	Presidential	major change
Spain	2004	2000	Legislative	major change
Spain	2008	2004	Legislative	no major change
Sweden	2002	1998	Legislative	no major change
Sweden	2006	2002	Legislative	major change
Switzerland	2003	1999	Legislative	no major change
Switzerland	2007	2003	Legislative	no major change
Taiwan	2001	1998	Presidential	major change
Taiwan	2004	2001	Presidential	no major change
Taiwan	2008	2004	Presidential	major change
Uruguay	2009	2004	Presidential	no major change
United Kingdom	2005	2001	Legislative	no major change
United States	2004	2000	Presidential	no major change
United States	2008	2004	Presidential	major change

Note: * all legislative elections in bicameral systems refer to the lower chamber, except Japan 2004 and Japan 2007 (upper house – Japanese House of Councillors – election)

At the operationalization level, Anderson et al. (2005) defined winner/loser status based on whether a citizen supported a given party before an election. This involves making an inference about dynamic effects with a static measure, by assuming that voters do not change their vote choice from one election to the next. The authors then aggregated the level of democratic satisfaction among the same group of voters and showed how the accumulation of their frustration over losing leads to declining democratic satisfaction. As we elaborate in the following, we relax this strict assumption on voting behaviour and use an alternative measurement to pin down the changes in winner/loser status between two consecutive elections. This better captures the effects of repeated losing, since it can differentiate repeated losers from the current losers who were previous winners but shifted their votes to a losing party in the current election. In other words, as done in Curini et al. (2012) and Chang et al. (2014), we can distinguish between four groups: two-time winners, past losers who are current winners, past winners who are current losers, and two-time losers.

Figure 3.1 shows the distribution of winner and losers between two consecutive elections in our dataset. It is clear from the graph that the percentage of two-time winners (WW) and two-time losers (LL) are roughly equivalent. The proportion of past winners who are current losers, and past losers who are current winners, is also similar. Interestingly, in countries that did not experience any major governmental change in the current election, only 26 per cent of respondents who were losers in the previous election emerged as winners in the current one. In contrast, in countries where a major governmental change took place, this percentage trebles to 58 per cent. This difference points to a well-known stability in voting behaviour. In other words, alternating winner/loser status is mostly attributable to changes in party fortunes rather than individuals switching parties from one election to the next.[7]

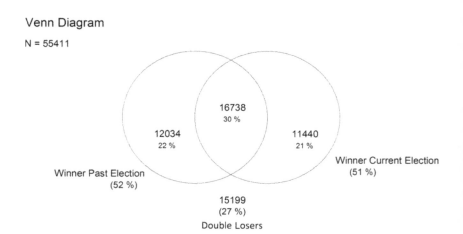

Figure 3.1 The distribution of past and present winner/loser status (%)

To test the impact of ideology, we construct the same PROXIMITY variable between voters and their government used in Chapter 2, but considering this time the ideological position of the first cabinet in the post-election moment. Similar to the previous chapter, Figure 3.2 reports the distribution of PROXIMITY for

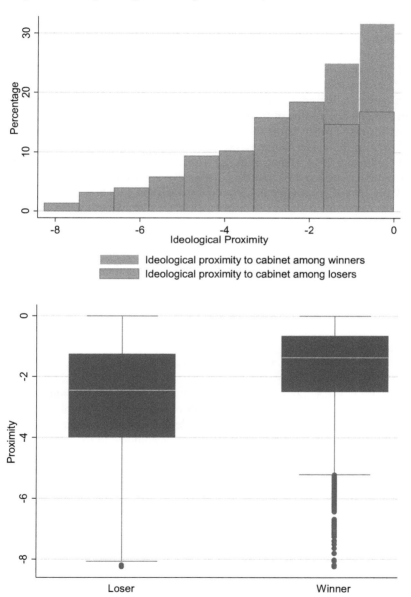

Figure 3.2 Citizen–government PROXIMITY by winner/loser status: overall distribution (upper panel) and box-plots (lower panel)

both present winners and losers. We can see a marked difference between the two groups: for present winners the mean value of PROXIMITY is −1.74, compared with −2.79 for present losers. At the same time, there is considerable variance within both groups.

Our dependent variable is respondents' level of satisfaction with democracy (SWD). Following a number of previous studies, this concept is captured by the question: 'On the whole, are you very satisfied (1), fairly satisfied (2), not very satisfied (3), or not at all satisfied (4) with the way democracy works in {country}?' In our sample, 8.2 per cent of respondents claimed to be not at all satisfied, 27.2 per cent not very satisfied, 53.7 per cent fairly satisfied and 10.9 per cent very satisfied. We collapsed these four categories into two to create a dummy variable that has a value of 0 when a respondent is not very satisfied or not at all satisfied, and 1 when he or she is fairly or very satisfied. This method is often followed in the extant literature (see Anderson and Guillory 1997; Armingeon and Guthmann 2014; Chang et al. 2014; Mebs and Nevitte 2002).[8] Our dependent variable, labelled SWD dummy, has an average value of 0.646, meaning that 64.6 per cent of our sample is fairly or very satisfied with how democracy works in their respective countries. However, there are considerable cross-country differences, with a value of SWD around 90 per cent in countries such as Denmark or Norway, compared with lower than 30 per cent in Bulgaria 2001, South Korea 2004 and Greece 2009 (see Figure 3.3).

The equation that we have estimated to test our hypotheses is as follows:

$$
\begin{aligned}
\text{logit}\left\{\Pr(y_{ij} \neq 0 | \mathbf{X}_{ij}, \mathbf{Z}_j)\right\} = {} & \alpha + \beta_1 (t_0 WINNER_{ij}) + \beta_2 PROXIMITY_{ij} \\
& + \beta_3 (t_0 WINNER_{ij}) + \beta_3 (t_0 WINNER_{ij}) * PROXIMITY_{ij} \\
& + \beta_4 (t_{-1} WINNER_{ij}) + \beta_5 (t_0 WINNER_{ij}) * (t_{-1} WINNER_{ij}) \\
& + \lambda \mathbf{X}_{ij} + \delta \mathbf{Z} + \zeta_j + \varepsilon_{ij} \qquad\qquad (3.1)
\end{aligned}
$$

where $\Pr(y_{ij} \neq 0 | \mathbf{X}_{ij}, \mathbf{Z}_j)$ is the probability that respondent i living in country j is satisfied with democracy given the set of independent variables included in our model; $t_0 WINNER_{ij}$ is a dummy variable that assumes a value of 1 if citizen i living in country j voted for a winning party/candidate in the current election; $PROXIMITY_{ij}$ is the variable that measures the ideological proximity between citizen i and the current government's position in country j; $t_{-1} WINNER_{ij}$ is a dummy variable that assumes a value of 1 if citizen i living in country j voted for a winning party/candidate in the previous election; all the other parameters are the same as in Chapter 2.

The two interaction terms presented in (3.1) are crucial for testing our hypotheses. In particular, according to Hypothesis 2, the marginal effect of being a current winner, that is $\partial(\text{Satisfaction with democracy})/\partial(t_0 Winner_{ij}) = \beta_1 + \beta_3 *$ $PROXIMITY_{ij}$, should increase (decrease) as the value of $PROXIMITY_{ij}$ increases (decreases). In other words, we expect a positive and significant β_3 coefficient. The second interaction term presented in (3.1), on the other hand, allows us to explore two possible alternative dynamic effects of winning. A significant and negative β_5

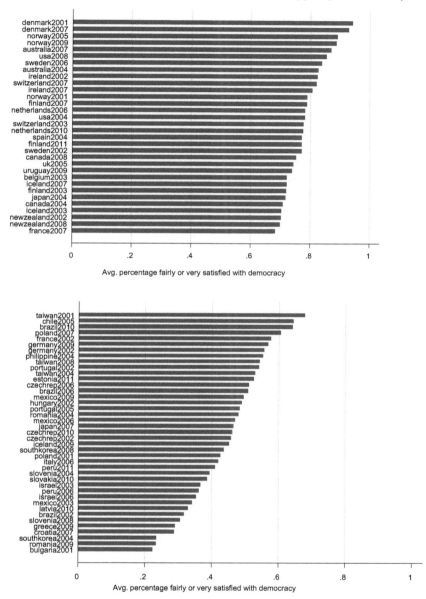

Figure 3.3 Satisfaction with democracy (average of 'very satisfied' plus 'fairly satisfied')

coefficient would alert us to the existence of a marginal dynamic impact, while any absolute dynamic impact should be highlighted by a positive and significant coefficient for β_1 and β_4 (with β_1 larger than β_4) and by a negligible magnitude (relative to β_1 and β_4) of β_5.

3.1   Control variables

It is necessary to control for a number of variables at both individual and country levels that have been found significant in the large empirical literature on the determinants of satisfaction with democracy (Canache et al. 2001; Mattes and Bratton 2007). At the micro level, in addition to socio-demographic factors (e.g. gender, age, age squared, education), we also include evaluations of the government's overall performance, to ensure that the winner/loser status variable is not simply a proxy for views toward the incumbent cabinet. The two remaining individual-level variables relate to respondents' general political and ideological attitudes. First, how much respondents believe that the people in power could make a difference reflects the extent to which they recognize democracy, especially elections, as meaningful. This belief in the intrinsic value of democracy, however, is distinct from opinions about how a democratic system functions in practice. To accurately test the latter, we should be cautious not to conflate it with the former.

Second, we create a dummy capturing the level of respondents' ideological extremity. This takes a value of 1 for those who position themselves on the extreme left or right along the ideological spectrum (i.e. lower than 2 or higher than 8 on a 0–10 left-right scale; around 18 per cent of our sample) and 0 otherwise, based on Anderson's argument that, 'given the general lack of ideological convergence toward the center' (Anderson 2010:222), these voters should be less satisfied with democracy. Moreover, including this variable ensures that the any effect found for PROXIMITY on SWD would be due entirely to citizen–government ideological proximity, rather than due to voters' own radical position.

At the aggregate (i.e. country) level, we included variables similar to those considered and already discussed in Chapter 2, namely:

a)   *Quality of formal institutions.* Institutions that promote the quality of resource allocation and provision of public good should increase satisfaction with democracy. As a proxy of such quality of formal institutions, we estimated once again the first factor of a principal components analysis on the World Bank's indices of quality of government. Higher values denote better quality.

b)   *Economic performance.* The worse a country's overall economic performance, the lower satisfaction with democracy should be. We include two economic indicators: the average GDP growth in the last five years and the deviation of GDP growth in the year immediately preceding the survey from this five-year average. This allows us to record the impact of last year's change in GDP above and beyond its contribution to the country's average GDP growth. These two variables allow us to differentiate between the short and medium-term economic impact on satisfaction with democracy.

c)   *Party system polarization.* Ezrow and Xezonakis (2011) showed that average levels of satisfaction with democracy are relatively low in countries with ideologically extreme party systems and offer the explanation that this due to a weaker representational link between elites and citizens. One can also expect that political debate in these countries would be characterized by antagonistic stances and refusal to compromise, with negative ramifications for government effectiveness. Indeed, studies have shown that party system polarization is related to cabinet survival (Warwick 1994), political stability (Sartori 1976), policy-making effectiveness (Tsebelis 2002) and to characteristics of policy representation (Abney et al. 2007; Huber and Powell 1994). Similar to Chapter 2, we use the index advanced by Dalton (2008) to measure party system polarization in each election.

d) *Majoritarian versus consensual decision-making.* We include a variable that captures the strength of institutional checks and balances (and therefore the diffusion of power) in each country, as well as the Gallagher index of disproportionality to account for the impact of electoral rules (Aarts and Thomassen 2008; Anderson 1998). Lijphart (1999) makes the point that consensual democracies outperform majoritarian ones in terms of responsiveness and do at least as well in terms of efficiency. This should lead to higher levels of satisfaction with democracy (Wagner et al. 2003). Similarly, Klingemann (1999) found that citizens in consensual democracies are significantly more satisfied than in majoritarian systems. Miller and Listhaug (1990) argued that a smaller number of parties (primarily deriving from disproportional electoral rules) is correlated with lower satisfaction with democracy because citizens have fewer choices. In other words, system support may be lower where electoral rules inhibit the emergence of new parties that represent new demands. Thus, we expect lower levels of satisfaction in countries where the Gallagher index is high.

Finally we also include a dummy that differentiates between *new* and *established democracies* according to the rule discussed in Chapter 2.

Table 3.3 lists all control variables included in our empirical analysis, along with their coding.

Table 3.3 Control variables and coding

Individual-Level Attributes	Coding Description
Age	actual age
Age squared	square of the above term
Gender	0 = female; 1 = male
Education	1= none; 8 = highest (completed university)
Government evaluation	1 = very good; 4 = very bad
Who in power makes difference	1 = makes a lot of difference; 5 = makes no difference at all
Ideological extremism (dummy)	1 = self-placement of 0, 1, 9, or 10 on 0–10 left-right scale
Country-Level Attributes	
Quality of institutions	higher score = better quality (first factor from principal component analysis of World Bank data)

(Continued)

Table 3.3 Continued

Individual-Level Attributes	Coding Description
Average GDP growth	average growth in past five years
Deviation from GDP growth	difference between the above term and GDP change in year preceding survey
Checks and balances	higher score = more institutional constraints (legislative chamber controlled by opposition party; number of parties in governing coalition)
New democracy (dummy)	1 = democracy in place for less than 25 years
Electoral rules	Gallagher index of disproportionality
Party system polarization	higher score = greater party system polarization

4.   Empirical findings: explaining satisfaction with democracy

Table 3.4 reports the results of the four models we estimated. The first is the familiar atheoretical model without Level 1 or Level 2 predictors, which allows us to decompose the total variance in our dependent variable between individual and country levels. In this case, country-level variance in our data explains around 20 per cent of the total variance, meaning that 20 per cent of the difference in levels of satisfaction with democracy is simply due to the fact that a respondent lives in one country rather than another. Given that the data are measured at the individual level, it is not surprising that variance at the country level is smaller than at the individual level (Steenbergen and Jones 2002).

Next, we turn to the question of how much our models can account for the variance in satisfaction with democracy, beginning with Model 1. Regarding the control variables at both individual and aggregate levels, the results largely accord with our expectations (with some exceptions that we will discuss later). At the individual level, respondents who are male, highly educated, and believe that it makes a difference who is in power are more likely to feel satisfied with democracy. In contrast, a negative assessment on government performance and ideological radicalism exert a significant and negative effect. Age has no significant impact.

At the aggregate level, the quality of formal institutions is positively related to satisfaction with democracy. The same holds true for economic performance, albeit only in the short-term: it is deviation from the mean GDP change, rather than average GDP growth, that turns out to be significant. Satisfaction is lower in new democracies, confirming that 'losers have not yet learned to lose in countries where democratic governance is of such recent vintage' (Anderson et al. 2005). The degree of party-system polarization decreases SWD, a finding probably attributable to the greater likelihood of either paralysis in policy-making or one

Table 3.4 Determinants of satisfaction with democracy

	(1)	*(2)*	*(3)*
	Null Model	*Model 1*	*Model 2*
Individual-Level Attributes			
t_0WINNER		0.547***	0.572***
		(0.044)	(0.106)
PROXIMITY		0.019*	0.018*
		(0.009)	(0.009)
PROXIMITY * t_0WINNER		0.039**	0.040**
		(0.013)	(0.013)
t_{-1}WINNER		0.206***	0.210***
		(0.032)	(0.032)
t_0WINNER * t_{-1}WINNER		−0.098*	−0.107*
		(0.048)	(0.049)
Extreme self-position		−0.121***	−0.123***
		(0.032)	(0.032)
Gender		0.108***	0.108***
		(0.021)	(0.021)
Age		−0.004	−0.004
		(0.004)	(0.004)
Age squared		0.000	0.000
		(0.000)	(0.000)
Education		0.048***	0.047***
		(0.006)	(0.006)
Government performance		−0.821***	−0.820***
		(0.015)	(0.015)
Who people vote make difference		0.151***	0.151***
		(0.009)	(0.009)
Country-Level Attributes			
New democracies		−0.380*	−0.376+
		(0.193)	(0.193)
Quality of institutions		0.231***	0.231***
		(0.041)	(0.041)
Average GDP growth		0.050	0.051
		(0.049)	(0.049)
Deviation of actual growth		0.049*	0.049*
		(0.019)	(0.019)
Party-system polarization		−0.137*	−0.136*
		(0.057)	(0.058)
Gallagher index		0.004	0.010
		(0.016)	(0.016)
t_0WINNER*Gallagher index			−0.016**
			(0.006)
Checks and balances		0.170**	0.161*
		(0.062)	(0.063)

(*Continued*)

Table 3.4 Continued

	(1)	(2)	(3)
	Null Model	*Model 1*	*Model 2*
t_0WINNER*Checks and balances			0.018
			(0.021)
Constant	0.558***	1.549***	1.544***
	(0.107)	(0.384)	(0.387)
St. Deviation at Level 2	0.911***	0.535***	0.534***
St. Deviation at Level 1	$\sqrt{\pi^2/3}$	$\sqrt{\pi^2/3}$	$\sqrt{\pi^2/3}$
Rho	0.202	0.080	0.081
Likelihood-ratio test variance at Level 2 = 0	8700.23***	2324.77***	2312.01***
N (Level 1)	55,411	55,411	55,411
N (Level 2)	73	73	73
AIC	63000.66	58056.83	58050.87
Log likelihood	−31498.331	−29007.417	−29002.435

Standard errors in parentheses; $^+ p < 0.10$, $^* p < 0.05$, $^{**} p < 0.01$, $^{***} p < 0.001$

camp imposing policies that intensely antagonize the opposing camp in countries where politics is highly polarized. Finally, the checks and balances variable is highly significant and positive as well, while the Gallagher index has little impact. Table 3.5 reports the expected impact of the control variables on SWD.

We can now turn to our main hypotheses. As previously discussed, the two interactive terms involving the t_0WINNER variable play a crucial role. Let us start with the hypothesis on the dynamic impact of being a winner. The highly significant (and negative) coefficient for the interaction term between t_0WINNER and t_{-1}WINNER clearly indicates the existence of a marginal dynamic impact. Figure 3.4 plots the marginal effect of winning in the past as a function of t_0WINNER on the probability of being satisfied with democracy, holding other independent variables (including PROXIMITY) at their means. The figure shows that winning in the previous election has a significant and positive effect on the probability of being satisfied with democracy, and this effect is stronger for current losers than two-time winners. Specifically, winning in the previous election when t_0WINNER = 0 increases the probability of being satisfied by 4.8 per cent, while this probability decreases to +2.2 per cent when t_0WINNER = 1.

Note that in Model 1, there is a second interaction term, t_0WINNER. To assess the true marginal effect of being a current winner (and its temporal dynamic: Brambor et al. 2006), we also need to control for the value of PROXIMITY, that is for the policy benefits of winning. This is shown in Figure 3.5, which depicts the marginal effect of being a current winner on the probability of feeling satisfied with democracy across the observed range of PROXIMITY in our dataset. Moreover, in Figure 3.5(a) we fix the value t_{-1}WINNER at zero, while in Figure 3.5(b) we consider respondents who are previous winners (i.e. t_{-1}WINNER = 1). We also

Table 3.5 Expected impact of all control variables on the probability of being satisfied with democracy

Control Variables	Expected Impact	95% c.i.	
Individual-Level Attributes			
Extreme self-position[a]	−2.7%	−4.1%	−1.3%
Who people vote makes difference[b]	+6.5%	+5.7%	+7.4%
Government performance[b]	−17.9%	−18.9%	−16.9%
Age (at age = 20)[c]	−0.5%	−1.4%	+0.4%
Age (at age = 50)[c]	−0.1%	−0.4%	+0.3%
Gender[a]	+2.4%	+1.5%	+3.2%
Education[b]	+3.1%	+2.3%	+3.9%
Country-Level Attributes			
New democracies[a]	−8.5%	−17.1%	−0.1%
Average GDP growth[b]	+2.1%	−1.8%	+6.1%
Deviation of actual growth[b]	+3.6%	+0.9%	+6.4%
Quality of institutions[b]	+15.7%	+10.5%	+20.9%
Party-system polarization[b]	−4.1%	−7.6%	−0.7%
Gallagher index[b]	+0.4%	−2.8%	+3.7%
Checks and balances[b]	+3.6%	+1.0%	+6.2%

Note: [a] expected impact by a unit increase; [b] expected impact of increasing the variable from first to third quartile of its sample distribution; [c] expected impact of increasing age of 10 years. The expected impacts are constructed using parameter estimates for Model 1 from Table 3.4 holding all other variables fixed at their means.

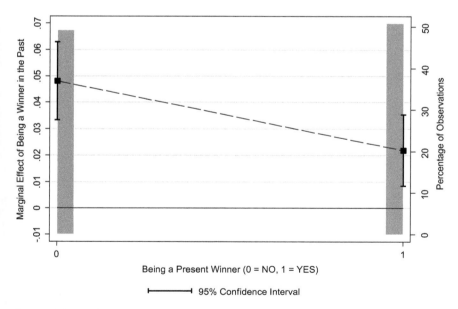

Figure 3.4 Marginal effect of winning in the previous election on SWD as the status of being a present winner changes

Note: The reported expected values and their corresponding confidence intervals are calculated via simulation using 10,000 draws from the estimated coefficient vector and variance–covariance matrix using the estimations of Model 1.

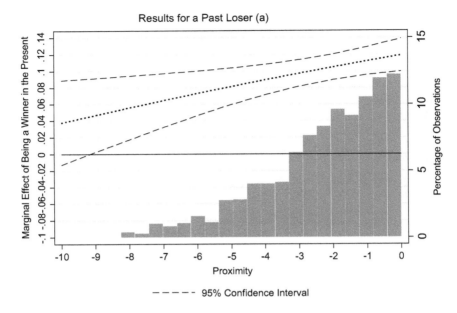

Results for a Past Loser (a)

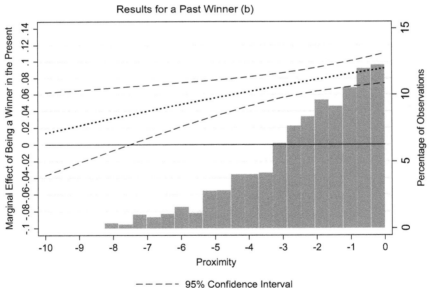

Results for a Past Winner (b)

Figure 3.5 Marginal effect of winning in the current election on SWD as PROXIMITY and winner/loser status in the previous election change

Note: The reported expected values and their corresponding confidence intervals are calculated via simulation using 10,000 draws from the estimated coefficient vector and variance–covariance matrix using the estimations of Model 1.

superimpose a histogram showing the frequency distribution for PROXIMITY over the marginal effect plots (the scale for the distribution is shown on the vertical axis on the right-hand side of the graph).

Figure 3.5 suggests the following conclusions. First, for both previous losers (Figure 3.5a) and previous winners (Figure 3.5b), the marginal effect of t_0WINNER on the probability of being satisfied with democracy increases as the value of PROXIMITY increases. Second, along the entire scale of PROXIMITY, the marginal effect of t_0WINNER is considerably higher for previous losers. For example, fixing PROXIMITY at −1, being a present winner (i.e. t_0WINNER = 1) increases the probability of being satisfied with democracy by 11.2 per cent among previous losers, compared with 8.5 per cent for repeated winners. This clearly confirms the marginal dynamic effect that we found in Figure 3.4 regarding t_{-1}WINNER. Third, for previous winners (Figure 3.5b), winning again starts to matter greatly in relative terms when PROXIMITY decreases greatly. To take an example: being a present winner does not increase the probability of being satisfied with democracy for any value of PROXIMITY lower than −7; it increases such probability by less than 5 per cent for any value of PROXIMITY between −5 than −7, but by as much as 8–9 per cent when PROXIMITY becomes greater than −2. This confirms our hypothesis that greater (lesser) ideological proximity between voters and the government can alleviate (exacerbate) the winner/loser disparity in satisfaction with democracy. In other words, for someone who has repeated experiences of winning, satisfaction with democracy would not be particularly boosted by yet another victory unless the ideologically position of the government comes very close to his or her own.

Here a sporting metaphor from English football may be appropriate: if the team you root for did not do well the last season, you would be happy to see its performance improving in the current season. However, if your team has won the previous Premier League, then the pleasure you get from watching the matches now depends on how well your team performs on the pitch. *Mutatis mutandis*, this also seems to apply to the relationship between satisfaction with democracy, a voter's experience as electoral winner, and the relative distance between his or her ideological position and that of his or her preferred party.

To conclude our analysis with the interaction terms, in Figure 3.6, we plot the marginal effect of PROXIMITY depending on t_0WINNER while holding all other variables at their means. This figure demonstrates that voter–government ideological proximity exerts a direct impact on satisfaction with democracy, irrespective of winner/loser status. If PROXIMITY increases from its first to its third quartile (i.e. from −3.25 to −0.85), the probability of being satisfied with democracy increases by 2.8 per cent for present winners. Doing the same for present losers has a weaker albeit still significant impact (+1.1 per cent). This direct relationship between ideological proximity and satisfaction with democracy corroborates the general theme of the book that the extent to which voter preferences are aligned with government policies makes a substantive difference, in this case with regard to how they feel about the political system. While the direction of causation may be intuitive, the magnitude of this effect, after controlling for a host of other factors, is noteworthy.

Having considered the result shown in Figures 3.4–3.6, we can now return to Hypothesis 1a, that is, the possibility of an *Absolute Dynamic Impact of winning*. This can be understood only by taking the possible mediating impact of PROXIMITY shown into account. Figure 3.7 simulates the predicted probability of being satisfied with democracy for the four possible combination of previous and current winners and losers (i.e. WW, WL, LW and LL) according to two values of PROXIMITY: −7 (i.e. an ideologically distant government) and −1 (i.e. a government ideologically close to the voter). The figure highlights two main implications. First, in both scenarios *Hypothesis 1a* is supported.[9] This happens because, for a two-time winner, the decreasing marginal utility in winning (i.e. the magnitude of the negative coefficient of the variable t_0WINNER $*$ t_{-1}WINNER) is not enough to offset the sum of the absolute impact of being a winner both in the past and in the present, (i.e. the positive betas of, respectively, t_0WINNER and t_{-1}WINNER) on SWD. This explains why the predicted probability of being satisfied for two-time winners is always larger than in the other cases. Moreover, the fact that WL is larger than LW suggests that voters who have only been a winner once seem to discount the impact of winning on satisfaction with democracy, though the difference is limited.[10]

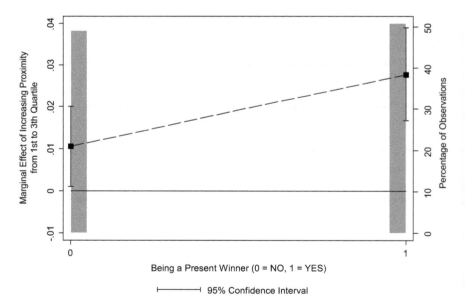

Figure 3.6 Marginal effect of PROXIMITY on SWD as the status of being a present winner changes

Note: The reported expected values and their corresponding confidence intervals are calculated via simulation using 10,000 draws from the estimated coefficient vector and variance–covariance matrix using the estimations of Model 1.

Note however that our analysis only considers data from two consecutive elections. We have just noted that in this scenario, the decreasing marginal utility in winning for a repeated winner in our model (see Figures 3.4 and 3.5) is still not enough to prevent the prevalence of the WW situation over all the others (see Figure 3.7). However, free elections should be considered as a set of repeated games where political actors compete with different probabilities of winning in each round. In this sense, we cannot exclude the possibility that over longer spans the marginal utility of (repeatedly) winning decreases so much as to render the experience of winning one more election on SWD negligible compared with a voter who rarely wins. If so, then a country with frequent government alternations presents the most favourable scenario in facilitating the diffusion of satisfaction with democracy, since a greater proportion of the electorate is likely to experience electoral victory at least once, either in the past or in the present. In other words, power alternation, besides restraining corruption and rent seeking (Milanovic et al. 2008; Sartori 1976), increasing economic growth (Feng 1997) and strengthening the rule of law (Horowitz et al. 2009), would also help to boost the overall level of satisfaction with democracy, although examination of data covering a longer time span is needed for a more thorough investigation of any cumulative effect of winning or losing.

The second finding highlighted by Figure 3.7 is that current losers may not necessarily have lower levels of democratic satisfaction once we take into account changes in their winner/loser status over time (i.e. if they were winners in the past)

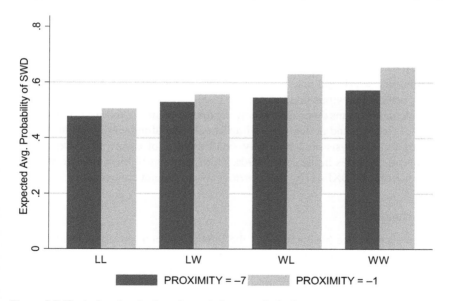

Figure 3.7 Exploring the absolute dynamic impact of winning

Note: The reported expected values and their corresponding confidence intervals are calculated via simulation using 10,000 draws from the estimated coefficient vector and variance–covariance matrix using the estimations of Model 1, holding all the other variables fixed at their means.

as well as the impact of PROXIMITY. This can be easily seen by contrasting the expected probability of SWD for current losers who are previous winners (LW) and are quite close to the current government (i.e. PROXIMITY = −1) and current winners who are previous losers (WL) and close to the current government (i.e. with a value of PROXIMITY = −7).

4.1 Robustness checks on the winner/loser effect

In the literature connecting the winner/loser effect with SWD, particular attention has been paid to the possible mediating impact of the institutional framework in which winning and losing takes place. For example, Anderson and Guillory (1997)[11] showed that opposition party supporters are likely to be less dissatisfied in consensual systems than their counterparts in presidential systems. The intuition is that even losers in consensual systems can influence policy to some extent, giving winners less absolute control than in majoritarian systems. We therefore introduce in Model 2 two new interaction terms involving t_0WINNER and, respectively, *checks and balances* and the *Gallagher index* (i.e. our two aforementioned proxies for consensual democracies). This allows us to check if the impact of t_0WINNER on satisfaction with democracy is mediated by the institutional context. Two things are worth noting here: first, the main coefficients that we have discussed up to now remain stable between Models 1 and 2, meaning that the relationship we found is quite robust. Second, the interaction between CHECKS and t_0WINNER is not significant, while the mediating impact of the Gallagher index on t_0WINNER is significant, but with an unexpected sign. That is, the impact of being a current winner on SWD is lower when the electoral system is less proportional, exactly the opposite result reported in Anderson and Guillory (1997) (see also Aarts and Thomassen 2008).

However, we should note three attenuating factors that may account for differences between previous findings and the results we report. First, it is possible that our interaction terms do not adequately capture Lijphart's consensual-majoritarian index.[12] Second, and perhaps more importantly, the aforementioned authors conducted their analysis on a relatively small number of cases (11) covering only European countries in the early 1990s. Third, we control for a number of factors (in particular PROXIMITY) that previous works did not control for.

Conclusion

In this chapter, we have examined the impact of voter–government ideological proximity and electoral winner/loser status on satisfaction with democracy, and demonstrated that the relationship between winner/loser status and satisfaction with democracy involves both absolute and marginal dynamics, as well as policy content. Our results show that winning once (either in the past or the present) always boosts satisfaction, and that current losers are not necessarily less satisfied, since they may have experienced winning in the past. Our findings also highlight the importance of ideological proximity. Being a winner today has a greater impact on democratic satisfaction for previous losers than those who have already won before. On the other hand, satisfaction increases among repeated winners only when they are ideologically close to the government. Ideological proximity also exerts a direct influence on democratic satisfaction for both winners and losers.

The finding concerning the importance of ideological proximity once again has crucial implications: governments that espouse policies which minimize the ideological distance between itself and a large proportion of citizens (including not just winners but also losers) can increase overall satisfaction with democracy in the population. By the same logic, an ideologically extreme government may lead to declining levels of political support. Assuming that electorates in most countries are congregated around the centre, our result highlights the virtue of having ideologically moderate governments, and also relates to Powell's (2000) proposition of gauging the quality of democracy by the distance between the government and the median voter.

As stated in the beginning of this chapter, we have analysed short-term, *specific* system support as theorized by Easton, which is more prone to fluctuate with the performance of political institutions and actors. We have not touched on the question of how ideological proximity or previous and current winner/loser status influences more abstract levels of political support identified by Norris. While one does not expect longer-term, *diffuse* support to vary within the limited temporal span covered by our analysis, it is conceivable that reiterated experiences of losing may not only affect assessment of contemporary governments and policies, but also jeopardize belief in the adequacy of the political system (i.e. democracy) itself. Such alienation could be compounded by wide ideological gulfs separating each government and repeated losers. This is a theoretical possibility that merit the attention of future studies.

Notes

1 One should note that governments can control legislative majorities based on a minority of votes. Consequently, losers can outnumber winners among the electorate.
2 We also follow the same approach for semi-presidential systems.
3 Once again, we analyse countries rated as free by Freedom House both at the time the election covered by the survey was held, and at the time of the previous election (this is necessary given that we compare the winner/loser effect in both the current and previous elections).
4 We did not include the following countries from CSES 3, given the lack of information needed to estimate several independent variables controlled for in our analysis: Chile 2009, Austria 2008, Portugal 2009, South Africa 2009, Spain 2008, Poland 2005, Germany 2005. For the same reason, we exclude the Netherlands 2002 from CSES 2. We have no information available with respect to our dependent variable in the Chile 2009 data. The information on vote choice in the previous election (needed to identify past winners and losers) is missing from the Austria 2008, Portugal 2009, South Africa 2009 and Spain 2008 data. Finally, the information needed to compute the variable labeled *"Who in power makes difference"* (see below) is missing in the Netherlands

2002, Poland 2005 and Germany 2005 data. Note that excluding the variable *"Who in power makes difference"* from our analysis, and adding these three surveys to the sample does not affect any of our conclusions.

5 We constructed the 'government change' variable reported in Table 3.2 from Keefer (2013). A 'major' government change happens each time the partisan composition of at least 40 per cent of the cabinet changes.

6 Where there were two rounds in presidential elections, we classify as winners citizens who reported voting for the winning candidate in the first round. Where the survey also contains information on the reported vote in the second round (in Brazil, France and Romania, but not in Chile and Peru), replicating the analysis by coding as winners citizens who voted for the winning candidate in the second ballot does not yield significantly different results. Unfortunately, detail on first and second ballot votes in the previous election is not available. In order to estimate respondents' past winner/loser status, we only include in our analysis respondents who meet voting age requirements in each country at the time of the previous election listed in Table 3.2.

7 To check the accuracy of the reported vote, we compared the aggregate distributions of actual and past election outcomes and recalled election outcomes. In both cases, we found that respondents tend to over-report voting for the winning parties or candidates, though the difference is not large. In the current election, 49.8 per cent of respondents reported voting for one of the governing parties, a figure slightly higher than the 46.9 per cent who actually voted for these parties. The equivalents for the previous elections are 50.6 per cent and 46.7 per cent, respectively.

8 Reher (2013) notes that collapsing the four original categories of SWD into a dichotomous measure helps to eliminate culturally based differences in the tendency to use extreme categories, and to avoid estimation problems due to empty cells. The alternative of using the original 4-point scale as the dependent variable, and employing an ordered logistic model, yields results that are very similar to the ones presented here.

9 This finding stands in contrast to that of Chang et al. (2014), who reported that it is the 'experience of being winners, not the current winner/loser status per se, that enhances voters' satisfaction with democracy.' In other words, these authors found the following lexicographic order: WW = WL = LW > LL. The difference with our results may be due to different sample sizes (Chang et al. 2014 analyse 12 electoral surveys, while we analyse 73 cases). Moreover, they do not control for several variables in our models including, crucially, voter–government PROXIMTY.

10 The 95 per cent confidence interval of each average expected probability never crosses each other.

11 See also Banducci and Karp (2003); Wells and Krieckhaus (2006).

12 Unfortunately the original index by Lijphart (1999) cannot be used for our analysis, since it refers to a previous time period (early 1990s) and does not include several new democracies covered by our study.

Appendix

The linkage between satisfaction with democracy and political participation

Given the results previously discussed, we are now in a position to answer the point left open at the end of Chapter 2. Recall that we noted the superior performance of radical (as compared with moderate) governments with respect to encouraging citizens' political participation. Should one count this against moderate governments? It is plausible to speculate that such governments are associated with lower levels of participation because on average citizens are more satisfied with how the political system functions. This is confirmed, albeit indirectly, in this chapter. While radical governments (i.e. more distant on average from the policy preference of most voters) are linked with greater propensity to engage in political activities (e.g. Chapter 2), they can cause a decline in satisfaction with democracy due to both direct and indirect (through winner/loser status) effects of citizen–government ideological proximity (e.g. Chapter 3). Putting the results in Chapters 2 and 3 together could then lead to the conclusion that ideologically

Table 3.6 The association between the index of political participation and satisfaction with democracy

	Model 1A
SWD	−0.039**
	(0.013)
Constant	0.871***
	(0.068)
St. Deviation at Level 2	0.399***
St. Deviation at Level 1	1.11***
Rho	0.114
Likelihood-ratio test variance at Level 2 = 0	3627.20***
N (Level 1)	38,770
N (Level 2)	35
AIC	118709.92
Log Likelihood	−59350.96

Standard errors in parentheses
$^{+} p < 0.10$, $^{*} p < 0.05$, $^{**} p < 0.01$, $^{***} p < 0.001$

moderate governments decrease participation because citizens are more satisfied with the way democracy works and hence have less need to articulate demands which are overlooked by policy makers.

Indeed, if we estimate what is admittedly a very basic model trying to explain the index of political actions (analysed in Chapter 2) by inserting satisfaction with democracy as an independent variable, we can see that respondents who are satisfied with democracy tend to participate less (Table 3.6). Given the structure of our data, we cannot rule out the possibility that it is the experience of political participation which influences democratic satisfaction rather than vice versa. Nevertheless, while not the main topic of this book, this is an intriguing finding that warrants a closer look in future research.

4 Ideological proximity and individual happiness

Introduction

The topic of life satisfaction – often used interchangeably with happiness – and its contributing factors have long been studied by economists (Bjørnskov et al. 2008; Blanchflower and Oswald 2004; Di Tella et al. 2001; Easterlin 1995, 2001; Frey and Stutzer 2000, 2002; Helliwell 2003; Ovaska and Takashima 2006), but have not drawn much attention from political scientists until relatively recently. At the macro level, Inglehart listed life satisfaction as an intrinsic part of political culture that reduces the potential for revolutionary change (1990:45). And from the perspective of ordinary citizens, the most direct and tangible means of judging the effectiveness of a given policy is whether it improves their lives. This prompts Layard to argue that 'the prime purpose of social science should be to discover what helps and hinders happiness' (2006:C32), while Tavits called on the political science profession to pay greater heed to 'the most fundamental goal of every citizen – to be happy' (2008:1607).

Several recent studies have examined the effect of political factors on life satisfaction, focusing mainly on country-level determinants such as institutional conditions (Bjørnskov et al. 2010), quality of governance (Helliwell and Huang 2008; Ott 2010) and policy outputs (Pacek and Radcliff 2008; Whiteley et al. 2010). In this respect, Álvarez-Díaz et al. concluded that 'politics emphatically does matter for . . . identifying the conditions that make human life rewarding' (2010:902).

However, concentrating on aggregate level variables may overlook the potential impact of individual attitudes vis-à-vis their governments on life satisfaction. The few studies that have explicitly investigated this topic mostly focus on the effect of *either* citizens' ideological self-positioning, to show that right-leaning individuals report higher levels of happiness (Tavits 2008; Taylor et al. 2006), *or* governments' ideological stances (Álvarez-Díaz et al. 2010; Di Tella and MacCulloch 2005).

In this chapter, we combine these two approaches by investigating the effect of both individual self-placements on the left-right spectrum and proximity to their government's position along the same scale. Furthermore, we depart from the existing literature by observing a contrast between moderate and radical citizens and its consequences for life satisfaction. As discussed later, this distinction turns out to be highly relevant both theoretically and empirically.

1.   Life satisfaction: definitions and determinants

The search for determinants of life satisfaction has generated a large volume of studies by economists, psychologists, and political scientists. Before discussing the literature, it is necessary to define what life satisfaction entails. According to Diener (1984), this term refers to 'a global assessment of one's life as a whole,' and such assessment is the result of a cognitive process. Some scholars use the term *subjective well-being* (SWB), and point out that SWB contains at least two distinct dimensions: life satisfaction and affect (Suh et al. 1998:484). However, since affect does not correlate highly with life satisfaction (Campbell et al. 1976), the present chapter will focus solely on the latter.

In addition to *life satisfaction*, many scholars also use the term *happiness*. While some studies have distinguished the two concepts, describing the former as cognitive, and the latter affective (see McKennell and Andrews 1980), other works treat them as measuring the same, or at least closely proximate, underlying notion (Veenhoven 1984; Wheeler 1991). Empirical analysis has confirmed 'a very strong congruence of both concepts' (Schyns 1998:11), suggesting that 'the two constructs may not differ' (Crooker and Near 1998:220). Thus, it is common to use happiness and life satisfaction interchangeably in the empirical literature (e.g. Bjørnskov 2003; Frey and Stutzer 2002), and we follow the same practice.[1]

Scholars have also discussed the validity of using responses to survey questions as an indicator of happiness (Diener 1984; Veenhoven 1993). While one may question whether national differences render subjective responses unreliable, Schnys (2002) found that survey questions on life satisfaction yield valid information, and Helliwell emphasized that this subjective measure 'produces a consistent set of forward-looking decisions and backward-looking evaluations' (2006:C35–36). These results confirm that 'reported subjective well-being is a satisfactory empirical approximation to individuality utility' (Frey and Stutzer 2002:408). Moreover, life satisfaction scores are comparable across countries (Veenhoven 2000) and not systematically biased due to social desirability (Konow and Earley 2008).

While studies on factors that contribute to happiness have examined a wide array of variables, these can be grouped into four broad categories. First, a number of *socio-demographic* factors are often identified as important influences on life satisfaction. For example, Blanchflower and Oswald (2004) reported that older and married citizens are more satisfied, while Bjørnskov et al. (2008) listed gender and the frequency of religious attendance among factors that significantly affect life satisfaction. The impact of religiosity is mentioned by Clark and Lelkes (2005).

Economic variables constitute the second set of factors influencing life satisfaction (Diener and Oishi 2000; Easterlin 1974, 1995). Many scholars have affirmed a positive link between income and life satisfaction (e.g. Diener and Diener 1995; Frey and Stutzer 2000), though this relationship is not always linear due to the 'diminished marginal utility of money' as one becomes richer (Veenhoven 1995:63). Thus, in affluent countries, changes in income exert only marginal influence on happiness (Helliwell 2006; Ovaska and Takashima 2006). Within countries, income makes a greater difference among the poor (Graham and Pettinato 2001). Additionally, it is often one's relative income that affects life satisfaction (Clark and Oswald 1996; Easterlin 1995, 2001; Layard 2006). Concerning other economic indicators, Schyns found GDP per capita as a significant predictor of life satisfaction across countries, though this effect disappears in sub-samples consisting of rich and poor nations only (1998:16–17). Ovaska and Takashima (2006) reported that while both GDP per capita and changes thereof influence levels of happiness, their impact is limited. Frey and Stutzer (2000) underlined that the unemployed tend to be significantly less satisfied with life.

The third set of factors affecting happiness comprises of individuals' *psychological traits*. It seems intuitive that personal attitudes and preferences would influence how individuals interpret information and thus form judgments about their conditions in life (Clore et al. 1994). Diener and Lucas surmised that personality or even genetic differences may exert an influence equal to or greater than external conditions such as economic circumstances (1999:214), and Emmons and Diener concluded that life satisfaction is driven by 'some combination of interpersonal competencies and internal states' such as self-esteem (1984:94). The impact of personality is not restricted to the individual level. Kahneman and Riis (2005) mentioned that aggregated personality differences may affect life satisfaction comparability across countries. Suh et al. (1998) identified different basis for judging life satisfaction, with societal norms playing a bigger role for assessment of subjective happiness for respondents in countries with 'collectivist' than 'individualist' cultures (see also Triandis 1995).

Lastly, *political factors* can influence life satisfaction. Most studies that pursue this line of research concentrated on comparing how regime and institutional differences across countries or sub-national regions affect citizens' level of happiness. Others emphasized institutional quality as a key contributor (Helliwell 2006; Ovaska and Takashima 2006). For instance, Helliwell and Huang (2008) pointed out that honest and efficient delivery of public services increase happiness in poor countries, while life satisfaction in rich countries depended more on the conduct of political and electoral institutions. Also, a number of scholars found that direct democracy raises life satisfaction (Budge 1996; Cronin 1989), because it allows citizens a greater say in monitoring and controlling policy outputs.[2]

In addition, scholars have investigated whether democracy itself influences life satisfaction. A number of studies confirmed a link between democracy or democratic values and happiness (Graham and Pettinato 2001). For example, Inglehart observed 'a remarkably consistent tendency for high levels of life satisfaction to go together with the persistence of democratic institutions over relatively long periods of time' (1990:41), and Dorn et al. (2005) reported that a country's Freedom House or Polity IV index score substantially affects its aggregate life satisfaction. In contrast, Bjørnskov et al. (2008) reached the opposite conclusion using both Polity IV scores and indicators of good governance such as freedom of the press and low corruption.[3]

2.   Ideological orientation and life satisfaction

Extant studies have mostly overlooked the (possible) impact played by individual-level ideological factors. Given that positive appraisal of policy procedures can increase life satisfaction (Helliwell and Huang 2008; Whiteley et al. 2010), it is natural to ask whether the relationship between policies and happiness is based solely on how much each citizen benefits from them, or also derives from his or her own policy preferences. If there is evidence for the latter claim, it would suggest that ideological orientation has an independent effect on life satisfaction. For example, Napier and Jost (2008) showed that right-leaning citizens in the United States are happier than those on the left (see also Taylor et al. 2006), and Tavits (2008) drew a similar conclusion in a cross-national study.

We can think of three possible explanations. First, ideological position may capture the effect of religion. People who place themselves toward the right tend to be more religious, and studies have shown that religiosity contributes to happiness (Frey and Stutzer 2002). Second, there may be an income effect, given positive correlations between ideology and income and between income and happiness. Finally, Napier and Jost (2008) propose a 'system justification theory perspective': someone who is happy with the existing social order would prefer an ideology that stresses its preservation (i.e. conservatism). Conversely, left-wing ideology, often associated with progressivism, is likely to attract people who seek changes to the status quo. Furthermore, citizens on different sides of the ideological divide may react differently to the same set of objective circumstances. For example, Malahy et al. (2009) found that in the face of economic inequality, life satisfaction remained unchanged for conservatives but declined for progressives, suggesting that the former may be happier because they are more ready to accept existing conditions.

Based on findings reported in these studies, we formulate our first hypothesis:

H1 (ideological position hypothesis): citizens with right-leaning ideological orientations report higher levels of happiness than those who place themselves on the left.

Another strand of literature puts the emphasis not on the left-right divide, but rather on a distinction between extreme and centrist ideological orientations, a point already discussed in Chapters 2 and 3. Several scholars noted as long as half a century ago that right- and left-wing extremists share a number of commonalities, such as authoritarian attitudes, dogmatism and radical methods of political engagement (Eysenck 1954; Rokeach 1960). McClosky and Chong pointed out that extremists on both ideological ends are characterized by resentment toward mainstream politicians and policies, and attraction to totalitarian measures (1985:343). Similarly, Greenberg and Jonas (2003) posited that, in addition to left versus right, there exists a separate ideological dimension pitting people who adhere rigidly to their views (radicals) against those who are more flexible (centrists). Other works showed that extremists are more cognitively sophisticated than centrists because they have greater need to justify their views (Kemmelmeier 2008; Sidanius 1985).[4]

Taken together, these findings suggest that the relationship between ideology and happiness may not simply be linear as proposed in H1, and lead to two opposite albeit equally plausible hypotheses which have not been tested before:

H2a (ideological extremism hypothesis): citizens holding ideologically extreme positions report lower levels of happiness than moderates due to their feeling of persecution and alienation.

H2b (ideological extremism hypothesis): citizens holding ideologically extreme positions report higher levels of happiness than moderates due to stronger belief in the veracity of their views.

If we assume that ideology plays a role in motivating governments' choice of policies, where a government is located along the left-right spectrum, and consequently what measures it seeks to carry out, can influence citizens' happiness. From a macro-level perspective, Álvarez-Díaz et al. (2010) showed that greater welfare spending and stricter regulatory policies lead to higher life satisfaction, and both Radcliff (2001) and Pacek and Radcliff (2008) argued that government intervention in the economy enhances satisfaction by bolstering a social safety net. These results imply that having leftist governments makes citizens happier. However, this is contradicted by other studies: Veenhoven reported 'no link between the size of the welfare state and the level of well-being within it' (2000:91), Tavits (2008) found no significant effect for social spending once other factors are controlled for, and Bjørnskov et al. (2007) even pointed out that excessive government consumption may actually lead to a decrease in overall life satisfaction. Thus, there is still no consensus on whether and how government ideology affects happiness.

In line with the theme of the book, we can further speculate that what matters for life satisfaction is not simply the ideological profile of governments per se, but rather, from the viewpoint of individual citizens, the relationship between their own preferences and those of their government. To the extent that a government's policies are predicated on its ideological stance, outputs may depend on which party is in power, *ceteris paribus*, and citizens would be happier with a government that pursues policies closer to their own preferences. Tavits (2008) showed that people who support parties in government (winners) express significantly greater satisfaction than those who voted for opposition parties (losers). Although Tavits did not focus on voter–government distance, insofar as ideological proximity predicts vote choice (see Adams et al. 2005), the two explanations partially overlap (remember our previous discussion in Chapter 2). Unfortunately, unlike the preceding chapters, we cannot control for respondents' vote choice in the following analysis since the dataset we use does not contain this information.[5]

This leads us to develop the following hypothesis:

H3 (ideological proximity hypothesis): The ideological proximity between citizens and their government is positively related to their level of happiness.

The topic of whether and how ideological proximity to the government affects citizens' life satisfaction has received little attention heretofore (but see Curini et al. 2014). Among the few exceptions, Di Tella and MacCulloch found that citizens are indeed substantially 'happier when the party in power has a similar ideological position to themselves' (2005:378). However, the impact of ideological proximity on life satisfaction was only tested indirectly through an interaction between individual self-placements and government positions. Moreover, respondents' ideological positions were collapsed into two broad categories (left and right), which precludes more sophisticated analysis on distinctions *within* each group and similarities *across* groups. Dreher and Öhler (2011) used a similar method, classifying governments as leftist, moderate or rightist, but did not find the same significant relationship between citizens' and governments' ideological positions. Finally, Taylor et al.'s (2006) study yielded the surprising finding that citizens' left-right orientation exerts greater influence on their life satisfaction when they live under a government from the opposite ideological camp.[6]

Part of the explanation for this unexpected result may lie in the distinction we made between citizens with moderate and radical ideological orientations. According to H2b, greater life satisfaction among radicals derives from a stronger belief in the correctness of their views. However, if their (hypothesized) higher level of happiness also derives from perceiving themselves as part of a minority (i.e. a 'purist' attitude), then anything that threatens this status (for example, a government closer to their own radical position) could make them less satisfied.

While only a speculative proposition, a quote from the Italian film *Caro Diario* (My beloved diary), winner for Best Director at the 1994 Cannes Film Festival, is illustrative in this regard. Nanni Moretti, the movie's director and protagonist, comments at one point (our translation from Italian): '*Do you know what I was thinking about? . . . that even by living in a society better than this one, I would always agree with a minority. . . . I believe in people, I just do not believe in the majority of people. I suspect that I will always feel myself more in my place, and be in agreement, with a minority.*'[7] This statement clearly highlights both the pride in identifying oneself as part of a minority and the reluctance to lose this status. This line of reasoning assumes that moderates base their subjective life satisfaction on *utilitarian* considerations, with an emphasis on concrete gains or losses resulting from certain policies, in contrast to extremists who derive happiness more on *expressive* grounds (Brennan and Lomasky 1993), and for whom abstract self-justifications matter more for life satisfaction.

Alternatively, it may be the case that radicals are more easily disappointed by contradictions between the stated goals of a supposedly ideologically proximate government and its actual policy performance. This could happen given that, compared with moderate governments, a (relatively) radical cabinet faces much greater external and internal constraints when trying to pursue its objective of altering the status quo, making citizens closer to this cabinet more likely to feel frustrated. This scenario involving expectations of large-scale transformation and subsequent disillusionment (see Stimson 1976) is less likely among centrist voters, precisely because they usually do not demand drastic changes to the status quo. The fact that niche (i.e. radical) parties on both sides of ideological spectrum tend to lose votes after participating in government (Buelens and Hino 2008; see also Deschouwer 2008; McDonnell and Newell 2011) offers an important, albeit indirect, evidence for both of the previous arguments.

Additionally, there is yet another possible explanation in countries with coalition governments. This involves ambivalence, defined as a situation in which an individual internalizes 'competing considerations relevant to evaluating an attitude object' (Lavine 2001: 915). Ambivalence is often measured toward a single object – an individual who has both strong positive and strong negative feelings about it is ambivalent – but has also been used to examine an individual's comparative ambivalence between parties and candidates (Basinger and Lavine 2005; Lavine 2001). Because a coalition requires citizens to consider more than one party when evaluating the government, it is a potential source of ambivalence. A voter is likely to evaluate each coalition member differently, and if these evaluations vary widely, for example, one party is greatly preferred or disliked over the other(s), he or she would be ambivalent toward the government. To relate this to our discussion, when a government is close to a radical voter, it is almost certain that the party he or she favours is included in the cabinet, but usually alongside other coalition partners. This can generate an ambivalent effect and cause the voter to be less happy if his or her distaste for other coalition members outweighs favourable attitudes toward his or her own preferred party.

Whether based on expressive rather than rational Downsian incentives, disappointed policy expectations or ambivalence toward coalition governments, the preceding paragraphs raise considerations not covered by H2b and H3. Consequently, we introduce the following two hypotheses that account for a conditional relationship between ideological proximity and citizens' self-placement on one hand, and life satisfaction on the other:

H4 (conditional ideological proximity hypothesis): for moderate citizens, the ideological proximity between citizens and their government is positively related to their level of happiness.

H5 (conditional ideological extremism hypothesis): citizens holding ideologically extreme positions report higher levels of happiness than moderates due to stronger belief in the veracity of their views. This gap increases as the ideological distance separating radical citizens from the cabinet increases.

As we will discuss later, *H4* and *H5* can be highly relevant for the overall impact on life satisfaction given certain governments' ideological positions.

3. Data and measurement

To test our hypotheses, we use individual-level measures of life satisfaction and ideological orientation obtained from the World Values Survey (WVS), which employs the same battery of questions across countries and time with respect to our main variables of interest. Five waves of the WVS are currently available (roughly 1980, 1990, 1995, 2000 and 2005), containing on average more than 1,000 respondents in each participating country. Our sample consists as usually of countries rated 'free' by Freedom House at the time of the survey, since fair and competitive elections are a prerequisite to analysing the relationship between the individual ideological positions, proximity to their governments, and happiness.[8] This leaves us with data from 40 countries, covering both established and new democracies, with an average of two surveys per country (Table 4.1). The total number of observations is around 70,000, the largest we could analyse without missing key variables.

Our dependent variable is respondents' level of satisfaction with life (SWL). In each survey, respondents are asked: 'All things considered, how satisfied are you with your life as a whole these days?' Response categories range from 'dissatisfied' (1) to 'satisfied' (10). The highest SWL scores are found in the Switzerland 1989 (8.4), Mexico 2005 (8.24) and Denmark 1981 (8.22) surveys, while the lowest scores are from three Eastern European countries: Bulgaria 1997 (4.81), Lithuania 1997 (5.03) and Estonia 1996 (5.12). The mean value in our sample is around 7.0, with a standard deviation of 2.1, which suggest considerable variation in SWL (Figure 4.1).

Respondents' ideological self-placement (labelled SELF) is measured on a 10-point scale, with lower values indicating more leftist orientations. To test the impact of voter–government proximity on life satisfaction, it is however also necessary to measure governments' ideological positions. Unlike the CSES surveys employed in the previous two chapters, the WVS surveys do not ask individual perceptions of parties' left-right locations, so cabinet position in each country is derived from a pool of six expert surveys: Benoit and Laver (2006), Castles and Mair (1984), Huber and Inglehart (1995), Wiesehomeier and Benoit (2009), the Chapel-Hill expert surveys (Steenbergen and Marks 2007), and for a few cases, the expert scores in the CSES dataset. In all cases, the position of the government in country i at the time j when the WVS survey was conducted is estimated, as done previously, as the average position of parties in government weighted by their respective seat share. We always select parties' scores from the expert survey temporally closest to the corresponding WVS wave to estimate government positions in each country. Finally, we normalize all the SELF and expert left-right scores on a 0–10 scale to allow for direct comparisons. From this, it is easy to estimate our usual PROXIMITY variable. In our sample, the average value of PROXIMITY is −8.2, with a standard deviation of 10.9.

3.1   Control variables

Of course, political variables are not the only determinants of happiness. Previous works have identified a number of socio-demographic and economic factors as important influences on life satisfaction. At the individual level, in addition

Table 4.1 List of countries included in Chapter 4

Country	WWS1	WWS2	WWS3	WWS4	WWS5
Argentina		1995	1999		
Australia		1995			2005
Austria		1990			
Belgium		1990			
Brazil					2006
Bulgaria			1997		
Canada	1982	1990		2000	2006
Cyprus					2006
Czech Republic			1998		
Denmark	1981	1990			
Estonia			1996		
Finland		1990	1996		2005
France	1981	1990			2006
Germany		1990	1997		2006
Great Britain	1981	1990			2005
Hungary		1991			
Iceland	1984	1990			
Ireland	1981	1990			
Italy	1981	1990			2005
Japan		1990		2000	2005
Lithuania			1997		
Mexico				2000	2005
Netherlands	1981	1990			2006
New Zealand			1998	2004	
Norway	1982	1990	1996		2007
Peru				2001	2006
Poland			1997		2005
Portugal		1990			
Romania					2005
Slovakia			1998		
Slovenia					2005
South Africa			1996		
South Korea				2001	2005
Spain	1981	1990	1995	2000	2007
Sweden	1982		1996		2006
Switzerland	1989		1996		2007
Taiwan					2006
Thailand					2007
United States		1990	1995	1999	
Uruguay			1996		

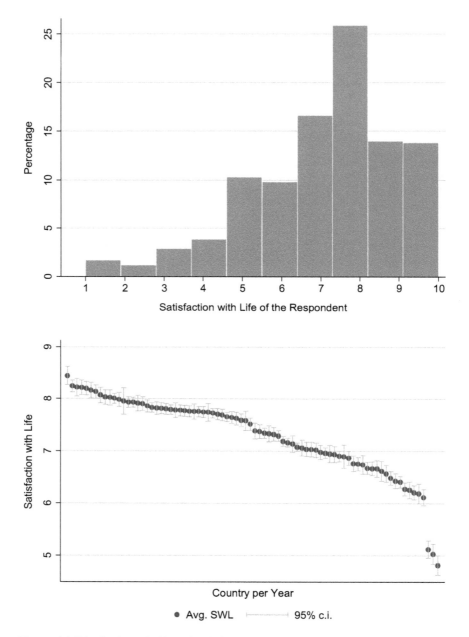

Figure 4.1 Distribution of citizens' satisfaction with life: overall (upper panel) and by country (lower panel)

to socio-demographic traits typically employed in the literature (e.g. *gender, marital status, age* and *age squared*, to account for the curvilinear relationship between age and life satisfaction), we include variables measuring respondents' self-reported *health*, given the strong correlation between this indicator and subjective well-being (Frey and Stutzer 2002), their level of generalized *trust* as a proxy for cognitive social capital (Helliwell 2003; Helliwell and Huang 2008), level of satisfaction with one's household *financial situation*, a dummy for parenthood (coded 1 for respondents with *children*) (Tavits 2008) and the *post-materialist* index included in the WVS.

Furthermore, we include two other variables that may mediate the relationship between ideological self-placement and happiness. First, *religion attendance* is used as a proxy for religiosity. Bjørnskov et al. (2008) listed the frequency of religious attendance as a factor that significantly affects life satisfaction. Second, many works have affirmed a positive relationship between personal income and life satisfaction (e.g. Diener and Diener 1995; Frey and Stutzer 2000). We measured the median income level in each country by employing a subjective answer on a country-specific 10-category income scale question, then created the dummy *income* variable that assumes the value of 1 if the respondent reports an above-median income in her country.[9]

Since our dataset covers 40 countries (and 80 countries * year), it is once again necessary to control for the impact of aggregate (i.e. country) level variables on individual life satisfaction. Concerning economic indicators, we included a country's average growth rate in the five years preceding each survey, assuming that the worse a country's recent economic performance, the lower life satisfaction would be. Given debates over the effect of gross domestic product (GDP) per capita as a predictor of life satisfaction across countries (see Schyns 2002), we used the logarithm of *GDP per capita*, estimated under purchasing power parity (PPP). Also, since Di Tella et al. (2001) and Frey and Stutzer (2000) underlined the significant negative impact of unemployment on life satisfaction, we controlled for a country's average unemployment rate in the five years preceding the survey.[10]

Following the previous discussion on macro-level variables, political institutions that enhance the quality of resource allocation and public goods provision should increase life satisfaction (Helliwell and Huang 2008). Recalling the procedure followed in the previous chapters, we thus include the first dimension scores extracted from a principal component analysis of the widely used World Bank governance indicators relating to effectiveness, regulatory efficiency, rule of law, lack of corruption, voice and accountability, and political stability (Kaufamn et al. 2002).[11]

We also include regional dummies for post-communist countries, Latin America and Asia, which previous works have shown to be highly significant (Bjørnskov et al. 2008, 2010). Besides controlling for similar cultural backgrounds, these dummies also largely correspond to regions with new democracies (with a few exceptions such as Japan).

Table 4.2 Control variables and coding

Variable	Coding Description
Individual-Level Attributes	
Age	
Age squared	squared value of Age
Gender	0 = female; 1 = male
Health	1 = very good; 4 = very poor
Post-materialism	1 = materialist; 2 = mixed; 3 = post-materialist
Financial satisfaction	1 = most dissatisfied; 10 = most satisfied
Marital status (dummy)	1 = married, widowed, or cohabiting; 0 otherwise
Parenthood (dummy)	1 = respondent has at least one child; 0 otherwise
Generalized trust	1 = most people can be trusted; 2 = can't be too careful
Income (dummy)	1 if respondent's income is above country-specific median; 0 otherwise
Religious attendance	1 = more than once a week; 8 = never
Country-Level Attributes	
Average GDP growth	Average GDP growth in the five years preceding survey year
Log of GDP per capita	Log of GDP per capita using PPP
Unemployment	Average unemployment rate in the five years preceding survey year
Quality of institutions	First dimension score from principal component analysis of World Bank governance indicators
Regional dummies	Dummies for Eastern Europe; Asia; South America
Period dummies	Dummies for each wave of the World Values Survey (first wave as omitted category

Finally, we add period fixed effects to the model (one dummy for each wave of WVS) to account for joint macro trends over time, such as business cycles, and of the changing country composition of our sample across waves (see Table 4.2 for a full list of control variables).

4. Empirical findings: explaining life satisfaction

Since our dependent variable (SWL) is on a 10-point scale, we use an ordered logistic model. In any ordered logistic model, an underlying score is estimated as a linear function of the independent variables and a set of cut points (or thresholds). Specifically, the formulation of a generic ordered logistic regression can be expressed as follows:

$$\text{logit}\left\{ \Pr(y_i > s | \mathbf{X}) \right\} = \beta \mathbf{X} + \varepsilon_i - k_s \tag{4.1}$$

where:
$\Pr(y_i > s | X)$ is the probability that respondent i reports a level of happiness higher than the threshold s given the model we are estimating, and k_s are the thresholds of

the ordered logit (nine in our case: that is, the number of categories of our dependent variable minus 1).

We are interested in identifying at which point of the latent scale the Category 1 changes to 2 (and similarly for the other categories). This is what we mean by a 'cutting point'. In particular, in all the subsequent analyses, our *benchmark score* will be the probability of moving above the cut point of 7, that is, the probability of being more satisfied than the average value in our sample. In addition, we have corrected standard errors in equation (4.1) for intra-group correlation and heteroskedasticity by clustering individuals at the country-year level (e.g. Spain 1981, Spain 1990, etc.).[12]

We also ran a sequential ordered logit (which relaxes the assumption of parallel regression of an ordered logit; see Boes and Winkelmann 2004).[13] All the qualitative results reported in the following hold intact. Moreover, the sequential ordered logit confirms that the categories of our dependent variable are monotonically related to an underlying latent variable, thus affirming that the ordered logistic model is appropriate.[14] Table 4.3 reports the four main models we estimated.

Table 4.3 Explaining life satisfaction

	Model 1	Model 2	Model 3	Model 4
Individual-Level Attributes				
PROXIMITY			0.0179	−0.00137
			(0.0119)	(0.0276)
SELF	0.0340***	−0.126***	−0.154***	−0.0764+
	(0.00538)	(0.0191)	(0.0281)	(0.0446)
SELF squared		0.0157***	0.0184***	0.00854*
		(0.00198)	(0.00276)	(0.00435)
Proximity*self-ideological position				0.0225*
				(0.0110)
Proximity*self-ideological position squared				−0.00286*
				(0.00122)
Income	−0.101***	−0.0961**	−0.0952**	−0.0916**
	(0.0304)	(0.0306)	(0.0305)	(0.0300)
Health	−0.530***	−0.531***	−0.531***	−0.531***
	(0.0221)	(0.0219)	(0.0219)	(0.0219)
Post-materialism	0.0410+	0.0368+	0.0375+	0.0385+
	(0.0209)	(0.0209)	(0.0209)	(0.0208)
Age	−0.0385***	−0.0386***	−0.0385***	−0.0384***
	(0.00376)	(0.00375)	(0.00375)	(0.00374)
Age squared	0.000405***	0.000402***	0.000402***	0.000401***
	(0.000038)	(0.000038)	(0.000038)	(0.000038)
Gender	−0.114***	−0.119***	−0.119***	−0.117***
	(0.0178)	(0.0175)	(0.0175)	(0.0174)
Financial satisfaction	0.402***	0.401***	0.401***	0.401***
	(0.0172)	(0.0172)	(0.0171)	(0.0171)

(Continued)

Table 4.3 Continued

	Model 1	Model 2	Model 3	Model 4
Religion attendance	−0.0340***	−0.0365***	−0.0363***	−0.0360***
	(0.00636)	(0.00644)	(0.00639)	(0.00635)
Generalized trust	−0.159***	−0.161***	−0.161***	−0.164***
	(0.0261)	(0.0259)	(0.0259)	(0.0256)
Marital status	0.380***	0.384***	0.384***	0.384***
	(0.0265)	(0.0267)	(0.0266)	(0.0266)
Parenthood	0.0874***	0.0876**	0.0873**	0.0863**
	(0.0264)	(0.0267)	(0.0266)	(0.0265)
Country–Year Attributes				
Log of GDP per capita	0.265+	0.245	0.245+	0.237
	(0.149)	(0.150)	(0.148)	(0.149)
Average GDP growth	0.0627**	0.0615**	0.0606**	0.0560**
	(0.0199)	(0.0197)	(0.0198)	(0.0202)
Unemployment	−0.0140+	−0.0146+	−0.0148+	−0.0148+
	(0.00831)	(0.00841)	(0.00834)	(0.00841)
Quality of institutions	0.0762	0.108	0.110	0.119
	(0.135)	(0.134)	(0.132)	(0.130)
Regional Dummies				
Asia	−0.596***	−0.578***	−0.571***	−0.562***
	(0.157)	(0.160)	(0.159)	(0.161)
Eastern Europe	−0.0356	−0.0382	−0.0227	−0.0103
	(0.147)	(0.148)	(0.149)	(0.151)
South America	0.649*	0.631*	0.634*	0.645*
	(0.292)	(0.292)	(0.289)	(0.280)
Period Dummies				
Wave 2	−0.189	−0.169	−0.173	−0.176
	(0.153)	(0.153)	(0.153)	(0.155)
Wave 3	−0.230	−0.205	−0.211	−0.231
	(0.175)	(0.175)	(0.174)	(0.177)
Wave 4	−0.314	−0.287	−0.292	−0.302
	(0.236)	(0.235)	(0.233)	(0.234)
Wave 5	−0.334	−0.309	−0.313	−0.317
	(0.219)	(0.220)	(0.219)	(0.221)
Observations	69705	69705	69705	69705
Pseudo R^2	0.100	0.101	0.101	0.102
AIC	251869.1	251610.5	251600.9	251562.7
Log likelihood	−125902.6	−125772.2	−125766.4	−125745.3
Chi squared	3253.7	3923.2	4361.8	4623.7
Country*Year	80	80	80	80
Country	40	40	40	40

Note: Clustered Standard errors over Country*Years in parentheses. Cut points suppressed to conserve space (available on request).

Source: WWS $^+ p < 0.10$, $^* p < 0.05$, $^{**} p < 0.01$, $^{***} p < 0.001$

Model 1 directly tests the *ideological position hypothesis* (H1). SELF has a highly significant and positive coefficient, corroborating findings in previous works that right-leaning citizens seem significantly more satisfied than their left-ist counterparts. Note that this is true after controlling for *income* and *religion attendance*, two of the main reasons advanced in the literature to explain this relationship. This suggests some deeper motivations behind the link between either wealth or religiosity and happiness. To explore this in more detail, we add in Model 2 a SELF-squared variable to check our alternative Hypothesis H2, namely the possibility of a curvilinear relationship between ideology and happiness. The results show that the squared term of SELF is significant and that Model 2 clearly improves upon Model 1 (as can be seen by comparing the AIC information criterion). As SELF increases, satisfaction decreases until it reaches a minimum at around 4, after which it increases again. Therefore, there is clearly stronger empirical support for Hypothesis H2b than H2a. In other words, respondents with ideologically extreme views appear to be happier than moderates.[15]

This is illustrated by Figure 4.2. We plot the probability of reporting a life satisfaction score above 7 as the value of SELF changes, holding all other variables fixed at their means, and also superimpose a histogram showing the frequency distribution of SELF (the scale is given by the vertical axis on the right-hand side of the graph). One can easily observe that Model 2 predicts a quadratic relationship.

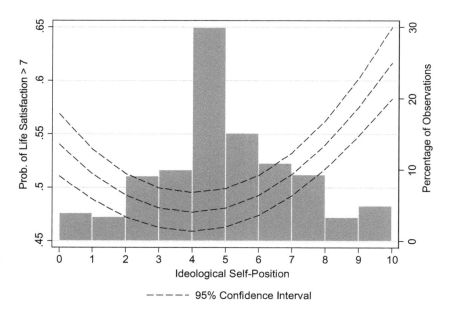

Figure 4.2 The impact of ideological self-placement on the benchmark score (i.e. the expected probability that life satisfaction is above the cut point of 7)

Note: The reported expected values and their corresponding confidence intervals are calculated via simulation using 10,000 draws from the estimated coefficient vector and variance–covariance matrix using the estimations of Model 2 from Table 4.3.

While it is true that conservatives are happier than progressives, as underlined in the literature, the most conspicuous pattern highlights that citizens at both extremes are more satisfied than centrists.

In Model 3, we introduce the PROXIMITY variable in order to test our *ideological proximity hypothesis* (H3). While this model is an improvement over Model 2, and the new variable has the expected positive sign, PROXIMITY fails to reach conventional statistical significance. This seems to challenge the central thesis of the book, namely the importance of citizen–government ideological distance. However, this is not the last word on the issue. As previously noted, both H4 and H5 assume a conditional relationship between ideological proximity and citizens' self-placements on one hand, and life satisfaction on the other. To properly test these two hypotheses, two interaction terms between SELF and PROXIMITY are added to our analysis, while assuming $\partial(SWL)/\partial(PROXIMITY)$ to be substantially higher (lower) for moderate (extreme) values of SELF. Conversely, we should expect that for citizens who place themselves on the extreme left or right, SELF would have a greater impact on SWL when PROXIMITY decreases.

We test this in Model 4, and results show that both interaction terms are highly significant, while the information criterion suggests that Model 4 improves on previous models. In order to understand the substantive magnitude of the effects found in Model 4, as well as the associated uncertainty, we simulate the marginal effect on our life satisfaction benchmark score by moving PROXIMITY from its first (−3.24) to third quartile (−0.940) as SELF changes. Figure 4.3 shows that, as

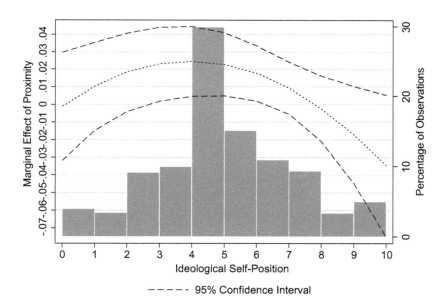

Figure 4.3 The marginal effect of PROXIMITY on the benchmark score as SELF changes

Note: The reported expected values and their corresponding confidence intervals are calculated via simulation using 10,000 draws from the estimated coefficient vector and variance–covariance matrix using the estimations of Model 4 from Table 4.3.

predicted by H4, while PROXIMITY does not exert a significant marginal effect for respondents professing ideological orientations on the two tails of the distribution (less than 3 and greater than 6), this factor makes a significant difference to moderate citizens. Furthermore, the magnitude of this effect is not insubstantial: for a respondent who placed himself or herself at 5, for example, the marginal effect of PROXIMITY increases our benchmark by 2.3 per cent, comparable to the impact of gender, parenthood or religious attendance (see Table 4.3).

The first three panels in Figure 4.4 replicate Figure 4.2 (i.e., the expected probability of reporting a life satisfaction score above 7 as the value of SELF changes) for three different values of PROXIMITY: at its minimum, average and maximum values. As H5 underscores, the curvilinear relationship between SELF and happiness changes its shape according to our expectation (more convex when PROXIMITY is low, more flat as PROXIMITY increases). To generalize this conclusion, in the lower-right panel of Figure 4.4, we report the marginal effect of a one-unit increase in SELF on our benchmark life satisfaction score as *both* SELF and PROXIMITY change.

The figure shows that this marginal impact is very large at extreme values of SELF when an individual is far away from the government position (i.e. low value of PROXIMITY). Indeed, at the negative extreme of PROXIMITY (−10), moving SELF from 0 to 1 (i.e. toward a slightly less radical position) decreases this

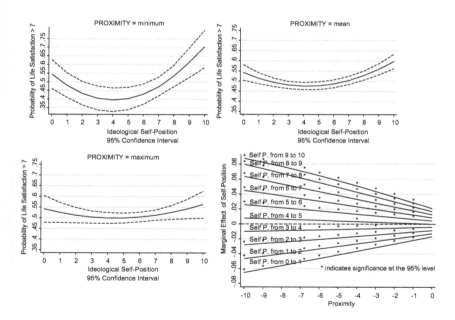

Figure 4.4 The marginal effect of ideological self-placement on the benchmark score as SELF as well as PROXIMITY changes

Note: The reported expected values and their corresponding confidence intervals are calculated via simulation using 10,000 draws from the estimated coefficient vector and variance–covariance matrix using the estimations of Model 4 from Table 4.3.

probability by 6 per cent, while moving SELF from 9 to 10 (i.e. becoming even more extreme) increases the probability by 8.8 per cent. In contrast, the same one-unit change for someone located in the ideological centre ground (SELF = 5) makes no significant difference to his or her level of happiness. At the same time, as PROXIMITY increases, the marginal impact of SELF at its extreme values also declines, exactly as H5 predicts. For example, when PROXIMITY equals 0, moving SELF from 0 to 1 decreases the probability by 1.6 per cent, while moving SELF from 9 to 10 increases it by 2.1 per cent.

Given that no government in our dataset is located at the extreme of either 0 or 10 on the left-right scale, the previous examples are only hypothetical scenarios. Nevertheless, this illustration is quite relevant when one focuses on the linkage between voters' and governments' ideological positions.

According to results in Model 4, an ideologically moderate government would make centrist voters, who constitute the vast majority of respondents in every country we analyse, (slightly) happier (Figure 4.3). Moreover, the same reaction would be found among extreme voters, given that they are by definition far away from a moderate government (as illustrated in Figure 4.4). In fact, the magnitude of this effect is larger than that for centrists. Conversely, an ideologically radical government would reduce satisfaction among centrist voters due to a large spatial distance, while having contrasting effects for extreme voters: a radical left government would make extreme right voters happier, while reducing satisfaction among extreme leftists (because the cabinet is located so close to themselves); the opposite occurs under a radical right government. This is summarized in Table 4.4, which suggests that a centrist government increases citizens' average level of happiness through a combination of the effects of ideological self-placement and citizen–government proximity.

Regarding the control variables, all the individual-level variables are significant and carry the expected sign, with one exception (Table 4.5). Life satisfaction appears to increase among respondents who are healthy, married, parents, women and satisfied with their financial situation, and those reporting higher generalized trust and more frequent religious attendance. In addition, happiness is higher among women and post-materialists (albeit only at the 90 per cent confidence interval in the latter case) and has an (anticipated) curvilinear relationship with age (reaching its minimum value at around 48 years).

On the other hand, we find a surprisingly significant and *negative* relationship between happiness and income: a person earning an above-median income

Table 4.4 The linkage between cabinet and voters ideological positions and its expected impact on the average level of happiness within a country

		Government's Ideological Position	
		Moderate	Extreme
Voters' Ideological Position	*Moderate*	+	—
	Extreme	+	+ and –

Table 4.5 Expected impact of the control variables on the benchmark score

Control Variables	Expected Impact	95% c.i.	
Individual-Level Attributes			
Income[a]	−2.3%	−3.8%	−0.8%
Health[b]	−25.9%	−27.9%	−23.9%
Post-materialism[b]	+1.9%	+0.002[+]	+0.037[+]
Age (at age = 20)[c]	−4.6%	−5.4%	−3.6%
Age (at age = 50)[c]	+1.4%	+0.9%	+2.0%
Gender[a]	−2.9%	−2.0%	−3.8%
Financial satisfaction[b]	+29.2%	+26.8%	+31.5%
Religious attendance[b]	−4.5%	−6.0%	−2.9%
Generalized trust[a]	−4.1%	−5.3%	−2.9%
Marital status[a]	+9.5%	+8.2%	+10.8%
Parenthood[a]	+2.2%	+0.9%	+3.5%
Country–Year Attributes			
Log of GDP per capita[b]	+5.3%	−1.3%	+11.8%
Average GDP growth[b]	+2.9%	+0.8%	+4.9%
Unemployment[b]	−2.0%	−0.039[+]	−0.001[+]
Quality of institutions[b]	+5.8%	−6.7%	+16.8%
Country Attributes			
Asia[a]	−13.5%	−20.6%	−6.0%
East Europe[a]	−0.2%	−7.6%	+7.2%
South America[a]	+15.6%	+2.2%	+28.0%
Temporal variables			
Wave 2[a]	−4.3%	−11.8%	+3.3%
Wave 3[a]	−5.6%	−13.9%	+2.8%
Wave 4[a]	−7.2%	−17.7%	+4.0%
Wave 5[a]	−7.8%	−18.1%	+3.1%

Note: [a]expected impact by a unit increase; [b]expected impact of increasing the variable from first to third quartile of its sample distribution; [c]expected impact of increasing age of 10 years; [+] 90 per cent confidence interval. The expected impacts are constructed using parameter estimates for Model 4 from Table 4.3 holding all other variables fixed at their means.

appears less happy than someone below this median. Why? One may speculate that the relationship between (personal) income and SWL is mediated by the context in which a person lives (see Clark et al. 2008). For example, Helliwell (2006) showed that changes in income exert only marginal influence on happiness in wealthy countries. Moreover, within countries, income makes a greater difference among the poor (Graham and Pettinato 2001). Thus, the sign of the income coefficient in Table 4.5 may be attributable to the fact that being wealthy matters more for happiness when a person lives in a relatively poor country than in a richer one.

To investigate this point in greater depth, we include an interaction between *income* and the log of *GDP per capita* in Model 5 (Table 4.6). Once again, the interaction term is significant, and it helps to partially clarify the puzzling result above. Figure 4.5 reports the marginal impact of *income* on our benchmark score. At the 90 per cent confidence interval, the marginal impact of *income* is positive and significant for low values of the log of GPD per capita (until around $3,000 per capita). However, as personal income increases, living in a rich country suppresses happiness among the wealthy. One possible explanation is that whereas rich individuals in poor nations are constantly reminded of their exceptional standing in comparison with their countrymen, there are more wealthy people in countries with higher GDPs per capita, and there tends to be frequent, perhaps even exclusive, interactions within this high-income circle. With their reference group confined to people of similar affluence, they may feel heightened motivation to acquire even greater wealth rather than satisfaction with their already sizeable fortune.

This is in line with the proposition that 'subjective well-being varies directly with income and *inversely with material aspirations*' (Easterlin 2001:481, italics added), and offers a partial answer to the famous 'Easterlin paradox', which refers to the fact that increases in wealth do not result in corresponding increases in levels of self-reported happiness, given that happiness is better envisioned as a product of relative rather than absolute wealth.

Note, moreover, that the interaction between *income* and the log of *GDP per capita* also allows us to better elucidate the impact on happiness of living in a rich country (Figure 4.6). According to Model 5, the marginal impact of increasing

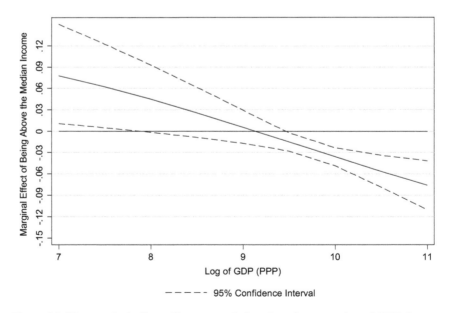

Figure 4.5 The marginal effect of income on the benchmark score as log of GDP changes

Note: The marginal effect plots are constructed using parameter estimates for Model 5 from Table 4.6. The confidence intervals are calculated via simulation using 10,000 draws from the estimated coefficient vector and variance–covariance matrix.

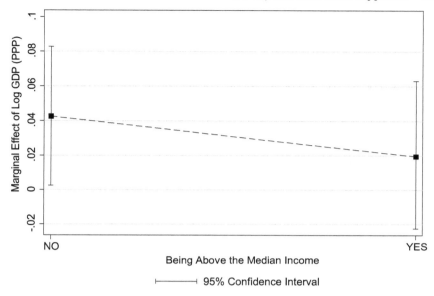

Figure 4.6 The marginal effect of log of GDP on the benchmark score as income changes

Note: The marginal effect plots are constructed using parameter estimates for Model 5 from Table 4.6. The confidence intervals are calculated via simulation using 10,000 draws from the estimated coefficient vector and variance–covariance matrix.

GDP per capita by one standard deviation (roughly US$10,000) on our benchmark is positive and statistically significant only among citizens with incomes lower than their national median (+5.5). In other words, as countries become more affluent, increasing national income makes the poor more satisfied (perhaps due to greater economic opportunities or more generous welfare), but has no effect for the wealthy. This is in line with previous findings (e.g. Dorn et al. 2005; Schnys 2002).

Concerning other macro-level control variables, one can see that satisfaction increases with improving economic trends (lower unemployment, higher GDP growth). Two of the three regional dummies are significant (positive for South America, negative for Asia), while period dummies are not.[16] Interestingly, the *Quality of Institutions* variable is never significant, contrary to Helliwell (2006). Helliwell and Huang (2008) also discussed the possibility that the impact of *Quality of Institution* is mediated by cross-national differences in wealth. We therefore add an interaction term between *Quality of Institution* and *GDP per capita* in Model 6. However, it does not turn out to be significant. This does not mean that the quality of institutions in a country does not matter for happiness. Rather, our analysis suggests that the effect of this factor is probably absorbed by its impact on economic variables. Indeed, if we re-run Model 6 without the three macro-economic variables, *Quality of Institution* becomes highly significant.[17]

Table 4.6 Explaining life satisfaction: robustness checks

	Model 5	Model 6	Model 7
Individual-Level Attributes			
Proximity	−0.00188	−0.00348	−0.00321
	(0.0274)	(0.0278)	(0.0225)
Self-ideological position	−0.0779+	−0.0716	−0.0749+
	(0.0443)	(0.0451)	(0.0435)
Self-ideological position squared	0.00873*	0.00823+	0.00853*
	(0.00432)	(0.00437)	(0.00435)
Proximity*self-ideological position	0.0223*	0.0234*	0.0226*
	(0.0109)	(0.0110)	(0.0109)
Proximity*self-ideological position squared	−0.00282*	−0.00291*	−0.00283*
	(0.00121)	(0.00122)	(0.00119)
Income	1.521*	−0.0912**	−0.0915**
	(0.651)	(0.0300)	(0.0300)
Income*log of GDP per capita	−0.167*		
	(0.0665)		
Health	−0.530***	−0.532***	−0.531***
	(0.0220)	(0.0217)	(0.0218)
Post-materialism	0.0379+	0.0401+	0.0388+
	(0.0207)	(0.0211)	(0.0212)
Age	−0.0380***	−0.0383***	−0.0384***
	(0.00380)	(0.00376)	(0.00374)
Age squared	0.000397***	0.000401***	0.000401***
	(0.000039)	(0.000038)	(0.000038)
Gender	−0.116***	−0.116***	−0.117***
	(0.0174)	(0.0174)	(0.0173)
Financial satisfaction	0.401***	0.401***	0.401***
	(0.0170)	(0.0171)	(0.0171)
Religious attendance	−0.0363***	−0.0363***	−0.0360***
	(0.00633)	(0.00623)	(0.00636)
Generalized trust	−0.169***	−0.171***	−0.164***
	(0.0243)	(0.0253)	(0.0255)
Marital status	0.392***	0.384***	0.384***
	(0.0258)	(0.0265)	(0.0267)
Parenthood	0.0857**	0.0884***	0.0862**
	(0.0262)	(0.0267)	(0.0265)
Country-Year Attributes			
Log of GDP per capita	0.310*	0.258	0.235
	(0.149)	(0.161)	(0.152)
Average GDP growth five years	0.0563**	0.0526*	0.0553*
	(0.0202)	(0.0207)	(0.0233)
Average unemployment five years	−0.0149+	−0.0169*	−0.0148+
	(0.00844)	(0.00837)	(0.00843)
Quality of institutions	0.120	1.288	0.120
	(0.130)	(1.188)	(0.130)

	Model 5	Model 6	Model 7
Quality of institutions*log of GDP per capita		−0.122	
		(0.125)	
Government ideological position			−0.00238
			(0.0221)
Regional Dummies			
Asia	−0.562***	−0.618***	−0.562***
	(0.162)	(0.181)	(0.161)
East Europe	−0.00960	−0.0522	−0.0106
	(0.151)	(0.156)	(0.152)
South America	0.651*	0.632*	0.646*
	(0.279)	(0.280)	(0.278)
Period Dummies			
Wave 2	−0.171	−0.109	−0.175
	(0.155)	(0.166)	(0.156)
Wave 3	−0.225	−0.129	−0.232
	(0.177)	(0.202)	(0.178)
Wave 4	−0.297	−0.173	−0.301
	(0.234)	(0.262)	(0.236)
Wave 5	−0.312	−0.184	−0.316
	(0.222)	(0.252)	(0.222)
Observations	69705	69705	69705
Pseudo R^2	0.102	0.102	0.102
AIC	251517.9	251543.4	251564.5
Log likelihood	−125722.0	−125734.7	−125745.3
Chi squared	3787.1	4472.8	4882.0
Country*Year	80	80	80
Country	40	40	40

Note: Clustered Standard errors over Country*Years in parentheses. Cut points suppressed to conserve space (available on request).

Source: WWS $^+ p < 0.10$, $^* p < 0.05$, $^{**} p < 0.01$, $^{***} p < 0.001$

In Model 7, finally, we introduce the variable *government ideological position* that controls for the ideological position of cabinets (i.e. $\overline{P}_j$ in equation [1] in Chapter 1). As noted, Radcliff (2001) and Pacek and Radcliff (2008) concluded that happiness is enhanced under governments which spend more on welfare. Here we take *government ideological position* as a proxy of welfare states/social spending. The results previously discussed regarding ideological self-placement and citizen–government proximity remain valid, while this new variable does not reach significance. The contrasting results may be due to the fact that previous studies did not take into account individual ideological orientations and citizen–government distance. Once these factors are controlled for, our analysis shows that the ideological positions of governments no longer exert an independent effect.

Conclusion

This chapter has investigated several hypotheses on the impact of ideology on individual life satisfaction. Do individual ideological orientations and voter–government congruence along the left-right spectrum really affect life satisfaction? In other words, does ideology matter for happiness at all? The answer is affirmative, with some notable caveats.

To summarize, there is a curvilinear relationship between ideological orientations and happiness, with those who locate themselves toward both extremes on the left-right scale feeling more satisfied than centrists. This challenges previous works which found a linear association, with higher levels of happiness among right-leaning citizens. Furthermore, we demonstrated that propinquity between self and government positions also contributes to happiness, but that this effect is heavily mediated by individual ideological orientation: centrists are more satisfied the closer they are to their government, while for citizens with radical views, proximity to government actually *diminishes* happiness.

This goes back once again to a leitmotiv of this book: ideologically moderate governments are better able to raise the overall level of happiness in society, since centrists far outnumber extremists in just about every country and the former profess higher levels of life satisfaction when their own positions are close to their government. On the other hand, citizens with more radical orientations may prefer the (self-)perception of isolated ideological purity, and care little about where the cabinet stands, so being distant from a moderate government does not make them less happy. In contrast, an extremist government would not only alienate the majority of voters who are centrists, but also fail to make more radical voters happier. In short, if we follow Bentham's utilitarian axiom that right and wrong is measured by the greatest happiness for the greatest number of people, then the key implication of our inquiry is this: a government with moderate policy orientations is *normatively* superior due to its positive effect on enhancing not only citizens' political system support (as shown in the previous chapter) but also their subjective well-being. We will return to such issue in the concluding chapter.

Findings in this chapter are also pertinent to academic and journalistic accounts on increasing political distrust among citizens in many advanced democracies, and the consequent rise in support for extreme parties (particularly the radical right) in some established democracies. Some mainstream parties may seek to contain a radical competitor by constraining the latter with responsibilities of government. Whatever the electoral payoff of such a strategy, this study suggests that it carries the risk of alienating large segments of the population, not only those with moderate views, but also core supporters of the said radical party, leading to a lose-lose situation with respect to life satisfaction among the citizenry. Finally, our results complement works that examine the failure of radical parties in government and offer a new perspective for future studies on the consequences of radical parties in office.

Notes

1 The World Value Survey (WVS) dataset used in our empirical analysis includes questions on both life satisfaction and happiness, with the two variables correlating at 0.5. Following Dreher and Öhler (2011), we use 'life satisfaction' since translation of the happiness item renders comparison of responses to this question more difficult. All findings reported below also hold true when the happiness variable is used.

2 This is sometimes referred to as 'procedural utility' (Frey and Stutzer 2002).

3 Part of this discrepancy may be due to different samples. For instance, Bjørnskov et al. (2010) found democracy contributing to happiness only in countries that have reached a certain level of economic development.

4 It has also been noted that citizens with more extreme attitudes, being more certain about the infallibility of their beliefs, are more predisposed to emotion-driven expressions of their views (Claassen 2007:373). This is relevant given the (largely positive) influence of individuals' emotional experiences on assessing life satisfaction (Suh et al. 1998).

5 Norris (2014) classified electoral winners and losers by matching individual responses to a question on which party they would support in the next general election with parties that entered government following the most recent election, but there are problems with this approach. Theoretically, the rather strong assumption that citizens' voting preferences are fixed may be questioned. Practically, two of the six waves of the survey used in our analysis did not ask which party respondents are likely to vote for.

6 For example, Republicans were 10–11 percentage points happier than Democrats during the Carter and Clinton administrations, but this margin was down to 3–5 per cent during the Reagan and first Bush presidencies (Taylor et al. 2006:5).

7 See http://www.youtube.com/watch?v=cvrRF6un-NU.

8 This choice is also data driven, given that reliable measures on the ideological position of governments in non-democratic countries are mostly unavailable.

9 Using the original income scale does not affect any of our findings.

10 In further testing, we included an individual level dummy that takes the value of 1 for unemployed respondents. All results hold intact, with this dummy having the expected negative sign. However, adding this variable would mean losing two country–year observations, so we decided to exclude it from the following analysis.

11 As already happens in Chapters 2 and 3, the six governance indicators load highly on one single underlying dimension (eigenvalue of the first factor is 5.3, explaining 88 per cent of total variance; the eigenvalue of the second factor is a mere 0.279). Including them in our analysis separately, or in some other combination (as done in Helliwell and Huang 2008), risks collinearity problems.

12 One potential criticism to our empirical strategy is that cluster-robust standard errors are asymptotic in the number of clusters (Golder and Lloyd 2014). Scholars differ on exactly how many clusters one needs to obtain reliable estimates. Wooldridge (2003:135) claims that problems can arise in some situations if the number of clusters is less than 40. Given that we have exactly 40 clusters in our sample, we feel reasonably safe.

13 According to the parallel regressions assumption, all the covariate effects in equation (4.1) are assumed to be constant across categories.

14 Clustering the standard errors for country only (i.e. Japan, Italy, etc.) does not substantially affect any of our findings. All results reported in the following remain intact when

our model is replicated using multilevel ordered logit. The same is true if we introduce fixed effects for each country.

15 In a further analysis, we have replicate Model 2 by including a variable measuring 'confidence in government', with responses ranging from 1 ('a great deal') to 3 ('not very much'). This variable indirectly taps the substantial content underlying Hypothesis H2a. According to Kim (2005), confidence in political institutions is a basic dimension of political alienation: people who resent mainstream politicians and policies should profess less 'confidence in government' and therefore, according to H2a, be less happy. In our replication, this variable turns out to be significant but with a positive coefficient, meaning that citizens with less confidence in government are actually happier. This result clearly contradicts H2a. On the other hand, the empirical support for H2b remains unaffected when the 'confidence in the government' variable is included. This supports H2b rather than H2a.

16 Excluding a number of new democracies (Argentina, Brazil, Mexico, Peru, South Africa, South Korea, Taiwan, Thailand) from the analysis due to concerns about their citizens' unfamiliarity with the left-right spectrum (Zechmeister 2006) does not affect the main findings of this study.

17 This may also be due to differences in country samples. Given the aim of our analysis, we did not consider non-democracies (many of them poor) covered in Helliwell and Huang's (2008) study. Moreover, we should note that the first observation for the World Bank governance indicators only became available in 1996. To arrive at measures for earlier periods in our dataset, we follow Helliwell and Huang (2008) by extrapolating the World Bank data from 1996 into the past, but there are questions about the validity of this method.

Conclusion

1. Government position, ideological proximity and their consequences

In the preceding chapters, we have argued that ideological proximity between citizens and their government can make an important difference with regard to various aspects of political attitudes and behaviour. Moreover, proximity not only exerts a direct impact, but is also relevant through its indirect mediating influence on citizens' electoral winner/loser status, as we have shown in Chapters 2 and 3, or on the self-ideological placement of voters, as illustrated in Chapter 4. Here we refer back to our starting point, Figure 1.1 in Chapter 1, and make additions to summarize our empirical findings about the impact of citizen–government proximity on three aspects of the democratic process. Ideological proximity enhances both satisfaction with democracy and subjective well-being, while exerting a negative influence on political participation (though not substantially on turnout) (Figure 5.1).

Consequently, one can say that all those factors that reduce the average value of ideological proximity in a country, that is, bringing citizens and their government closer together, have a positive impact on two noteworthy aspects of the political process: evaluations of how democracy works, and how happy people feel with their lives. We have already seen one such factor: as noted in Chapter 1, ideologically radical governments are eccentric (given that a large majority of citizens in most countries congregate around the ideological centre: see Figure 1.7). For similar reasons, the more ideologically eccentric a cabinet is, the larger the citizen–government gap becomes (Figure 1.6).

We now want to tackle this issue explicitly. Let's use the label AVG_PROXIMITY for the average value of citizen–government PROXIMITY in each country covered in this book.[1] We want to see the relationship between this value and the respective national *government ideological* position. From our preceding analysis, we expect a non-linear relationship between *government ideological* position and AVG_PROXIMITY in a given country that resembles an inverted U: that is, low values of AVG_PROXIMITY if the government occupies a relatively radical position, and higher values as the government moves toward the centre. Therefore,

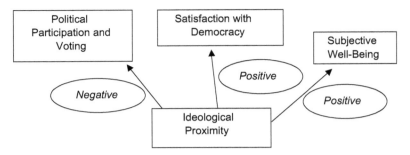

Figure 5.1 The impact of citizen–government ideological proximity

Table 5.1 The determinants of AVG_PROXIMITY

	Model 1
Government position	1.470***
	(0.111)
Government position squared	−0.145***
	(0.010)
Constant	−5.605***
	(0.278)
St. Deviation at Level 2	0.184***
St. Deviation at Level 1	0.327***
Rho	0.241
Likelihood-ratio test variance at Level 2 = 0	15.96***
N (Level 1)	197
N (Level 2)	46
AIC	166.00
Log likelihood	−78.00

Standard errors in parentheses; $^+ p < 0.10$, $^* p < 0.05$, $^{**} p < 0.01$, $^{***} p < 0.001$

besides the variable *government ideological* position, we also include in the following analysis the squared value of this variable. Table 5.1 reports our empirical model. Note that we have 197 observations from 46 countries. Given that there is sometimes more than one observation per country in this dataset, we employ a linear multilevel model, as we have done in Chapter 2.

As Table 5.1 shows, the relationship between *government ideological position* and AVG_PROXIMITY is not only significant, but also quite substantial: as *government ideological position* increases, so does AVG_PROXIMITY until it reaches a minimum around 5.1 on the 0–10 left-right scale. After passing this point, AVG_PROXIMITY starts to decrease markedly as *government ideological position* increases (Figure 5.2).

We have previously noted how the ideological position of a given government, through its impact on PROXIMITY, could affect aspects of political attitude and

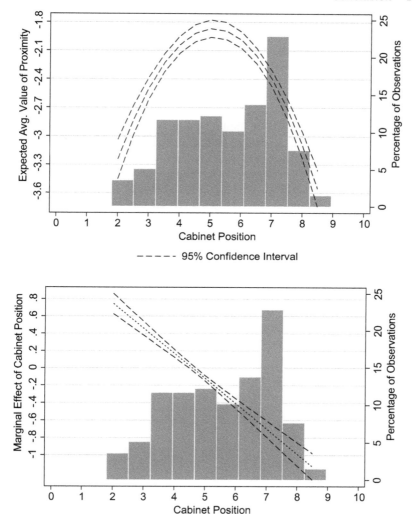

Figure 5.2 The impact of government ideological position on the expected value of AVG_PROXIMITY (upper panel) and its marginal effect (lower panel)

Note: The reported expected values and their corresponding confidence intervals are calculated via simulation using 10,000 draws from the estimated coefficient vector and variance–covariance matrix using the estimations of Model 1 from Table 5.1.

behaviour. Now we can quantify the magnitude of this impact. According to the Model in Table 5.1, when a government adopts a relatively centrist position (a position of 5.1 on a 0–10 left-right ideological scale), it tends to greatly increase AVG_PROXIMITY overall. In this respect, the four panels of Figure 5.3 report, respectively, the marginal impact on the probability of *participating, voting,* expressing a high level of *satisfaction with democracy* and a probability of *life satisfaction* being higher than 7 (i.e. our benchmark score; see Chapter 4), illustrated by an 'ordinary' citizen when the government shifts from a moderate position (5.1 on the 0–10 left-right scale) over the entire possible range of the ideological spectrum.

More formally, the probabilities reported in Figure 5.3 are constructed using parameter estimates for Model 4 in Table 2.4 with respect to political participation (Chapter 2)[2], for Model 6 in Table 2.6 with respect to voting (Chapter 2), for Model 1 in Table 3.4 with respect to satisfaction with democracy (Chapter 3), and for Model 4 in Table 4.3 with respect to life satisfaction (Chapter 4). In the figure, we also superimpose a histogram in each panel showing the frequency distribution of governments' ideological positions in the sample analysed in each chapter (the scale of the distribution is given by the vertical axis on the right-hand side of the graphs).[3]

With the expected exception of election turnout, our counterfactual scenarios always show that it makes a big difference whether governments occupy a relatively moderate or radical position. For example, when a cabinet assumes a value of 2 on the left-right scale, we expect a decrease of 1.3 per cent in the probability of being satisfied with democracy compared to the baseline category (i.e. a government positioned at 5.1). How relevant is this finding? If we compare the impact of a government's ideological shift with economic indicators, for example, then the previous change yields an effect that is roughly equivalent to improving

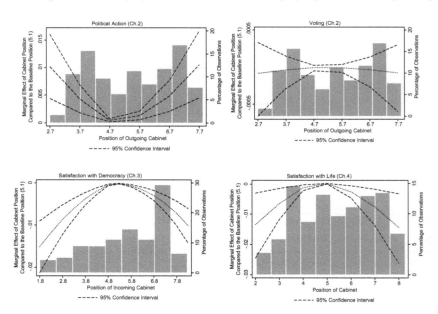

Figure 5.3 Counter-factual scenarios: what happens to the probability of being involved in political participation, in voting, satisfied with democracy and satisfied with life, given changes in government position over the left-right scale (baseline cabinet position: 5.1)

the short-term economic growth of a country relative to its trend (i.e. deviation from actual gross domestic product [GDP] growth) by 2 per cent. This is far from negligible.

A similar story can be told with regard to life satisfaction. Indeed, if we compare the impact of a government's ideological shift with changes in a country's rate of GDP growth, for example, then moving a government's position from a moderate 5.1 to a radical 2 produces a negative impact on happiness roughly equivalent to a 1.4 per cent decrease in the average GDP over five years.

In contrast, as governments become more radical, the probability of political participation increases: for example, when all the cabinets assumes a value of 3 on the left-right scale, we expect the probability of taking part in at least one mode of political action to *increase* by around 1 per cent compared to a government located at 5.1. While not insubstantial, such an increase is less dramatic than the changes in levels of democratic system support and happiness that a similar shift in government position would bring about. Moreover, as noted in the Appendix to Chapter 3, ideologically moderate cabinets may discourage political participation because citizens are more satisfied with the way democracy works.

2. Closing remarks: does virtue lie in the middle?

A fundamental tenet of democracy is that governments are supposed to reflect the policy preferences of their citizens (Dahl 1956; Pitkin 1967). A more specific, and now widely accepted, formulation of this principle is that 'policy congruence is . . . the criterion for good representation' (Andeweg 2011:50). In most studies of political representation, the primary touchstone for 'good representation' is that elected politicians act in accordance with the preferences of their electorate, which many cross-sectional studies referred to as 'policy (or issue- or ideological-) congruence'. In longitudinal studies, this criterion is often called 'policy responsiveness', with scholars debating whether some representative institutions adapt to changes in public opinion more quickly than others (Stimson et al. 1995), and whether responsiveness is the result of representatives adapting to voters, or the other way around (Esaiasson and Holmberg 1996; Holmberg 1997). All these studies agree that policy congruence (or responsiveness) is an indicator of good political representation.

Questions on how well government reflects the values and preferences of ordinary citizens have therefore long been discussed and debated. Such questions are fundamental to the principle and practice of democracy, and the search for adequate answers will – deservedly – continue to occupy the attention of both practitioners and scholars. For example, are proportional electoral rules better able to yield such 'congruence' (i.e. 'proximity' as used throughout this book) compared to majoritarian ones? Or vice versa? There is an extensive literature on the issue (for contrasting results, see for example Golder and Lloyd 2014; Golder and Stramsky 2010; Huber and Powell 1994; Powell and Vanberg 2000) and the debate seems set to continue.

That said, instead of inserting ourselves into this ongoing discussion, this book is an attempt to take one step beyond it: rather than examining factors that facilitate policy proximity between citizens and their government, we set out to explore the possible ramifications of congruence. In other words, instead of asking 'what makes governments more representative?', we have looked for answers to the question 'so what if governments are (or are not) representative?'

This inquiry has taken us through different aspects of political attitudes and behaviour. If our findings can be summarized in a single sentence, it would be as follows: results of empirical analyses suggest that, when considering the ideological position of a given government, *in medium stat prŏpinquum*, therefore *in medium stat virtus*. Governments located around the middle of the ideological spectrum have the effect of enhancing not only citizens' evaluation of how democracy works, but also their sense of personal well-being. The causal mechanisms differ for self-identified moderates and radicals, but the combined effect confirms that virtue does indeed lie in the middle.

Given that a majority of the populace in almost every country congregate around the centre of the left-right spectrum, the counterfactual scenarios illustrated above point at the significant negative impact of an ideologically radical government due to its distance (i.e. lack of proximity) from most citizens. Furthermore, the preceding chapters have also shown that those espousing more extreme views do not see their level of satisfaction with democracy and subjective well-being increase in the rare cases when their government's position approaches their own. If anything, proximity produces quite the contrary effect: the closer they are to their government, the *less* satisfied they feel. We have speculated on possible rationales behind this seemingly counter-intuitive result. Whatever the reason may be, this reinforces our conclusion that, as far as citizen attitudes are concerned, governing from the centre yields a much more salutary outcome than doing so from either fringe of the ideological spectrum.

In view of this, we can introduce a new element to the discussion on the suitability of different institutional arrangements for producing citizen–government congruence. According to Aarts and Thomassen (2008), the key question in the debate between the majoritarian and consensus models should simply be which one serves democracy best. Following the findings presented in this book, we argue that rather than taking citizen–government congruence as the basis for judging different models of democracy, an alternative standard can be the extent to which each model facilitates political participation, support for the democratic system of governance, or a sense of individual well-being. While the ideological distance between citizens and their governments is a significant variable in affecting each of these dimensions, the topics we have examined are by no means exhaustive. We hope that our effort only serves as a starting point for further research on the importance and effects and citizen–government proximity.

Notes

1 Golder and Stramsky (2010) argued that there are several ways to think about congruence between citizens and their representatives. First, there is 'one-to-one' congruence

between some summary of voter ideal points (for example, the ideal point of the median voter on some policy dimension) and some summary of policy positions on offer (the government's position on the same dimension). Second, there is 'many-to-one' congruence between the full set of voter ideal points and some summary of policy positions on offer. Finally, there is 'many-to-many' congruence between the full set of ideal points and the full set of policy positions arising from party competition (e.g. the set of elected legislators' ideal points). According to the 'many-to-one' measure, congruence is high when the average absolute distance between citizens and the representative is small. Now, if you replacing 'representative' with the government, yields the AVG_PROXIMITY variable discussed in the text.

2 We have decided to focus on Model 4 in Table 2.4 rather than Model 3 when we talk about political participation, given the former model is estimated through a logit model. This allows us to directly compare the counterfactual results here reported in terms of probabilities. The results reported are unaffected in their substantial implications if the latter parameters are used.

3 The simulation uses as always 10,000 draws from the estimated coefficient vector and variance–covariance matrix from each of the models quote above.

References

Aarts, K., and J. J. Thomassen (2008) 'Satisfaction with democracy: Do institutions matter?' *Electoral Studies*, 27, 1: 5–18.

Abney, R., A. Morrison, and G. Stradiotto (2007) 'On the stability of representation: A cross-national study of the dispersion of parties' policy positions in plurality and proportional representation systems', *Representation*, 43, 3: 151–165.

Adams, J. (2001) *Party Competition and Responsible Party Government: A Theory of Spatial Competition Based Upon Insights from Behavioral Voting Research*, Ann Arbor: University of Michigan Press.

Adams, J. F., S. Merill, and B. Grofman (2005) *A Unified Theory of Party Competition. A Cross-National Analysis Integrating Spatial and Behavioral Factors*, Cambridge, UK: Cambridge University Press.

Adorno, T. W., E. Frenkel-Brunswik, D. J. Levison, and N. R. Sanford (1950) *The Authoritarian Personality*. New York: Harper and Row.

Aldrich, J. N. (1983) 'A Downsian spatial model with party activism', *American Political Science Review*, 77: 974–990.

Aldrich, J. N. (1995) *Why Parties*, Chicago: University of Chicago Press.

Alesina, A., R. Di Tella, and R. MacCulloch (2004) 'Inequality and happiness: Are Europeans and Americans different?' *Journal of Public Economics*, 88, 9–10: 2009–2042.

Almond, G., and S. Verba (1963) *The Civic Culture: Political Attitudes and Democracy in Five Nation*, Princeton, NJ: Princeton University Press.

Alvarez, M. R., and J. Nagler (2004) 'Party system compactness: Measurement and consequences', *Political Analysis*, 12, 1: 46–62.

Álvarez-Díaz, Á., L. González, and B. Radcliff (2010) 'The politics of happiness: On the political determinants of quality of life in the American states', *Journal of Politics*, 72, 3: 894–905.

Anderson, C. J. (1998) 'Parties, party systems, and satisfaction with democratic performance in the new Europe', *Political Studies*, 46, 3: 572–588.

Anderson, C. J. (2010) 'Electoral supply, median voters, and feelings of representation in democracies', in R. J. Dalton and C. J. Anderson (eds.), *Citizens, Context, and Choice*, Oxford, UK: Oxford University Press.

Anderson, C. J., A. Blais, S. Bowler, T. Donovan, and O. Listhaug (2005) *Losers' Consent: Elections and Democratic Legitimacy*, Oxford, UK: Oxford University Press.

Anderson, C. J., and C. A. Guillory (1997) 'Political institutions and satisfaction with democracy: A cross-national analysis of consensus and majoritarian systems', *American Political Science Review*, 91, 1: 66–81.

Anderson, C. J., and A. J. LoTempio (2002) 'Winning, losing and political trust in America', *British Journal of Political Science*, 32: 335–351.

Anderson, C. J., and M. M. Singer (2008) 'The sensitive left and the impervious right: multilevel models and the politics of inequality, ideology, and legitimacy in Europe', *Comparative Political Studies*, 41, 4–5: 564–599.

Anderson, C. J., and Y. V. Tverdova (2001) 'Winners, losers, and attitudes about government in contemporary democracies', *International Political Science Review*, 22, 4: 321–338.

Andeweg, R. B. (2011) 'Approaching perfect policy congruence: Measurement, development, and relevance for political representation', in M. Rosema, B. Denters, and K. Aarts (eds.), *How Democracy Works*, Amsterdam: Pallas.

Armingeon, K., and K. Guthmann (2014) 'Democracy in crisis? The declining support for national democracy in European countries, 2007–2011', *European Journal of Political Research*, 53, 3: 423–442.

Banducci, S. A., and J. A. Karp (2003) 'How elections change the way citizens view the political system: Campaigns, media effects and electoral outcomes in comparative perspective', *British Journal of Political Science*, 33, 3: 443–467.

Barber, B. (1984) *Strong Democracy: Participatory Politics for a New Age*, Los Angeles: University of California Press.

Barnes, S. H. (1977) *Representation in Italy. Institutionalized Tradition and Electoral Choice*, Chicago: University of Chicago Press.

Basinger, S. J., and H. Lavine (2005) 'Ambivalence, information, and electoral choice', *American Political Science Review*, 99, 2: 169–184.

Beck, T., G. Clarke, A. Groff, P. Keefer, and P. Walsh (2001) 'New tools in comparative political economy: The database of political institutions', *World Bank Economic Review*, 15, 1: 165–176.

Bellucci, P., and V. Memoli (2013) 'The determinants of democratic support in Europe', in P. C. Magalhaes, D. Sanders, and G. Toka (eds.), *Citizens and the European Polity: Mass Attitudes Towards the European and National Polities*, Oxford, UK: Oxford University Press.

Benoit, K., and M. Laver (2006) *Party Policy in Modern Democracies*, London: Routledge.

Bjørnskov, C. (2003) 'The happy few: Cross-country evidence on social capital and life satisfaction', *Kyklos*, 56, 1: 3–16.

Bjørnskov, C., A. Dreher, and J.A.V. Fischer (2007) 'The bigger the better? Evidence of the effect of government size on life satisfaction around the world', *Public Choice*, 130, 3–4: 267–292.

Bjørnskov, C., A. Dreher, and J.A.V. Fischer (2008) 'Cross-country determinants of life satisfaction: Exploring different determinants across groups in society', *Social Choice and Welfare*, 30: 119–173.

Bjørnskov, C., A. Dreher, and J.A.V. Justina (2010) 'Formal institutions and subjective well-being: Revisiting the cross-country evidence', *European Journal of Political Economy*, 26, 4: 419–430.

Blais, A., and R. K. Carty (1990) 'Does proportional representation foster voter turnout?' *European Journal of Political Research*, 18, 2: 167–181.

Blais, A., and F. Gelineau (2007) 'Winning, losing and satisfaction with democracy', *Political Studies*, 55, 2: 425–441.

Blais, A., E. Gidengil, R. Nadeau, and N. Nevitte (2001) 'Measuring party identification: Britain, Canada and the United States', *Political Behavior*, 23, 1: 5–22.

Blanchflower, D.G., and A.J. Oswald (2004) 'Well-being over time in Britain and the USA', *Journal of Public Economics*, 88, 7: 1359–1386.

Boes, S., and R. Winkelmann (2004) 'Income and happiness: New results from generalized threshold and sequential models', *IZA Discussion Paper* No. 1175.

Bok, D. (2010) *The Politics of Happiness*, Princeton, NJ: Princeton University Press.

Bourne, P.A. (2010) 'Unconventional political participation in a middle-income developing country', *Current Research Journal of Social Sciences*, 2, 3: 196–203.

Bowler, S., and J.A. Karp (2004) 'Politicians, scandals, and trust in government', *Political Behavior*, 26, 3: 271–287.

Brambor, T., W. Clark, and M. Golder (2006) 'Understanding interaction models: Improving empirical analyses', *Political Analysis*, 14, 1: 63–82.

Brennan, G., and L. Lomasky (1993) *Democracy and Decision: The Pure Theory of Electoral Preference*, Cambridge, UK: Cambridge University Press

Budge, I. (1994) 'A new spatial theory of party competition: Uncertainty, ideology and policy equilibria viewed comparatively and temporarily', *British Journal of Political Science*, 24, 3: 443–467.

Budge, I. (1996) *The New Challenge of Direct Democracy*, Cambridge, UK: Polity Press.

Budge, I., I. Crewe, and D. Farlie (eds.) (1976) *Party Identification and Beyond: Representations of Voting and Party Competition*, London: Wiley.

Budge, I., H.-D. Klingemann, A. Volkens, J. Bara, and E. Tanenbaum (eds.) (2001) *Mapping policy preferences: Estimates for parties, electors, and governments 1945–1998*, Oxford, UK: Oxford University Press.

Budge, I, and D. Robertson (1987) 'Do parties differ and how? Comparative discriminant and factor analyses', in I. Budge, D. Robertson, and D. Hearl (eds.), *Ideology, Strategy and Party Change. Spatial Analyses of Post-War Election Programmes in 19 Democracies*, Cambridge, UK: Cambridge University Press.

Buelens, J., and A. Hino (2008) 'The electoral fate of new parties in government', in K. Deschouwer (ed.), *New Parties in Government: In Power for the First Time*, London: Routledge.

Calvo, E., and T. Hellwig (2011) 'Centripetal and centrifugal incentives under different electoral systems', *American Journal of Political Science*, 55, 1: 27–41.

Campbell, A., P.E. Converse, W.E. Miller, and D. Stokes (1960) *The American Voter*, Chicago: Chicago University Press.

Campbell, A., P.E. Converse, and W.L. Rodgers (1976) *The Quality of American Life: Perceptions, Evaluations, and Satisfactions*. New York: Russell Sage Foundation.

Canache, D., J.J. Mondak, and M.A. Seligson (2001) 'Meaning and measurement in cross-national research on satisfaction with democracy', *Public Opinion Quarterly*, 65, 4: 506–528.

Carney, D.R., J.T. Jost, S.D. Gosling, and J. Potter (2008) 'The secret lives of liberals and conservatives: Personality profiles, interaction styles, and the things they leave behind', Political Psychology, 29. 6: 807–840.

Castillo, A.M.J. (2006) 'Institutional performance and satisfaction with democracy: A comparative analysis', Paper presented at the *Comparative Studies of the Electoral System Plenary*, Seville, March.

Castles, F.G., and P. Mair (1984) 'Left–right political scales: Some 'expert' judgments', *European Journal of Political Research*, 12, 1: 73–88.

Chang, E., Y.-H. Chu, and W.-C. Wu (2014) 'Consenting to lose or expecting to win? Inter-temporal changes in voters' winner-loser status and satisfaction with democracy', in J.J. Thomassen (ed.), *Election and Democracy*. Oxford, UK: Oxford University Press.

Cho, W., and M. Bratton (2006) 'Electoral institutions, partisan status, and political support in Lesotho', Electoral Studies, 25, 4: 731–750.

Claassen, R. L. (2007) 'Campaign activism and the spatial model: Getting beyond extremism to explain policy motivated participation', *Political Behavior*, 29, 3: 369–390.

Clark, A., and O. Lelkes (2005) 'Deliver us from evil: Religion as insurance', Paris-Jourdan Sciences Economiques Working Paper No.2005–43.

Clark, A. E., and A. J. Oswald (1996) 'Satisfaction and comparison income', *Journal of Public Economics*, 61, 3: 359–381.

Clark, A., P. Frijters, and M. A. Shields (2008) 'Relative income, happiness and utility: An explanation for the Easterlin paradox and other puzzles', *Journal of Economics Literature*, 46, 1: 95–144.

Clinton, J., S. Jackman, and D. Rivers (2004) 'The statistical analysis of roll call data', *American Political Science Review*, 98, 2: 355–370.

Clore, G. L., N. Schwarz, and M. Conway (1994) 'Affective causes and consequences of social information processing', in R. S. Wyer and T. K. Srull (eds.), *Handbook of Social Cognition*, Hillsdale, NJ: Erlbaum

Cox, G. W. (1990) 'Centripetal and centrifugal incentives in electoral systems', *American Journal of Political Science*, 34, 4: 903–935.

Criado, H., and F. Herreros (2007) 'Political support taking into account the institutional context', *Comparative Political Studies*, 40, 12: 1511–1532.

Cronin, T. E. (1989) *Direct Democracy: The Politics of Initiative, Referendum, and Recall*. Cambridge, MA: Harvard University Press

Crooker, K. J., and J. P. Near (1998) 'Happiness and satisfaction: Measures of affect and cognition?' *Social Indicators Research*, 44, 2: 195–224.

Curini, L. (2010) 'Experts' political preferences and their impact on ideological bias', *Party Politics*, 16, 3: 299–321.

Curini, L. (2011) 'Government survival the Italian way: The core and the advantages of policy immobilism during the First Republic', *European Journal of Political Research*, 50, 1: 110–142.

Curini, L. (2015) 'The conditional ideological inducement to campaign on character valence issues in multiparty systems. The case of corruption', *Comparative Political Studies*, 48(2): 168–192.

Curini L., and P. Martelli (2010) 'Ideological proximity and valence competition. Negative campaigning through allegation of corruption in the Italian legislative arena from 1946 to 1994', *Electoral Studies*, 29, 4: 636–647.

Curini, L., and F. Zucchini (2010) 'Testing the theories of law making in a parliamentary democracy: A roll call analysis of the Italian Chamber of Deputies (1987–2006)', in T. Konig, G. Tsebelis, and M. Debus (eds.), *Reform Processes and Policy Change: Veto Players and Decision-Making in Modern Democracies*, Berlin: Springer.

Curini, L., and F. Zucchini (2012) 'Government alternation and legislative party unity: The case of Italy, 1988–2008', *West European Politics*, 35, 4: 826–846.

Curini, L., W. Jou, and V. Memoli (2012) 'Satisfaction with democracy and the winner-loser debate: The role of policy preferences and past experience', *British Journal of Political Science,* 42, 2: 241–261.

Curini, L., W. Jou, and V. Memoli (2014) 'How moderates and extremists find happiness: Ideological orientation, citizen-government proximity, and life satisfaction', *International Political Science Review,* 35, 2: 129–152.

Dahl, R. A. (1956) *A Preface to Democratic Theory*, Chicago: University of Chicago Press.

Dahl, R. (1971) *Polyarchy: Participation and Opposition*, New Haven, CT: Yale University Press.

Dalton, R.J. (1985) 'Political parties and political representation: Party supporters and party elites in nine nations', *Comparative Political Studies*, 18, 3: 267–299.

Dalton, R.J. (1999) 'Political support in advanced industrial democracies', in P. Norris (ed.), *Critical Citizens*, Oxford, UK: Oxford University Press.

Dalton, R.J. (2004) *Democratic Challenges, Democratic Choices: The Erosion of Political Support in Advanced Industrial Democracies*, Oxford, UK: Oxford University Press.

Dalton, R.J. (2006) 'Social modernization and the end of ideology debate: Patterns of ideological polarization', *Japanese Journal of Political Science*, 7, 1: 1–22.

Dalton, R.J. (2008) 'The quantity and the quality of party systems: Party system polarization, its measurement, and its consequences', *Comparative Political Studies*, 41, 7: 899–920.

Dalton, R.J., and M.P. Wattenberg (2000) *Parties without partisans: Political Change in Advanced Industrial Democracies*, Oxford, UK: Oxford University Press.

Dalton, R.J., A. Van Sickle, and S. Weldon (2010) 'The individual–institutional nexus of protest behaviour', *British Journal of Political Science*, 40, 1: 51–73.

Dawes, C.T., P. Jo. Loewen, and J.H. Fowler (2011) 'Social preferences and political participation', *Journal of Politics*, 73, 3: 845–856.

Dennis, J., and D. Owen (2001) 'Popular satisfaction with the party system and representative democracy in the United States', *International Political Science Review*, 22, 4: 399–415.

Deschouwer, K. (ed.) (2008) *New Parties in Government: In Power for the First Time*, London: Routledge.

Devos, T., D. Spini, and S.H. Schwartz (2002) 'Conflicts among human values and trust in institutions', *British Journal of Social Psychology*, 41, 4: 481–494.

Di Tella, R., and R. MacCulloch (2005) 'Partisan social happiness', *Review of Economic Studies*, 72, 2: 367–393

Di Tella, R., R.J. MacCulloch, and A.J. Oswald (2001), 'Preferences over inflation and unemployment: Evidence from surveys of happiness', *American Economic Review*, 91: 335–341.

Diamond L., and L. Morlino (2005) *Assessing the Quality of Democracy*, Baltimore: The Johns Hopkins University Press.

Diener, E. (1984) 'Subjective well-being', *Psychological Bulletin*, 95, 3: 542–575.

Diener, E., and M. Diener (1995) 'Cross-cultural correlates of life satisfaction and self-esteem', *Journal of Personality and Social Psychology*, 68: 653–663.

Diener, E., and S. Oishi (2000) 'Money and happiness: Income and subjective well-being across nations', in E. Diener and E.M. Suh (eds.), *Culture and Subjective Well-Being*, Cambridge, MA: MIT Press

Dorn, D., J.A.V. Fischer, G. Kirchgässner, and A. Sousa-Poza (2005) 'Democracy and happiness revisited', Presented at the European Public Choice Society Conference, Durham, 31 March–3 April.

Downs, A. (1957) *An Economic Theory of Democracy*, New York: Harper and Row.

Dreher, A., and H. Öhler (2011) 'Does government ideology affect personal happiness? A test', *Economics Letters*, 111, 2: 161–165.

Duch, R.M., J. May, and D. Armstrong (2010) 'Coalition-directed voting in multi-party democracies', *American Political Science Review*, 104, 4: 698–719.

Easterlin, R.A. (1974) 'Does economic growth improve the human lot?', in P.A. David and M.W. Reder (eds.), *Nations and Households in Economic Growth*, New York: Academic Press.

Easterlin, R.A. (1995) 'Will raising the incomes of all increase the happiness of all?', *Journal of Economic Behavior and Organization*, 27, 1: 35–47.

Easterlin, R. A. (2001) 'Income and happiness: Towards a unified theory', *Economic Journal*, 111: 465–484.

Easton, D. (1965) *A System Analysis of Politics*, New York: Harper.

Easton, D. (1975) 'A re-assessment of the concept of political support', *British Journal of Political Science*, 5, 4: 435–457.

Emmons, R. A., and E. Diener (1985). 'Personality correlates of subjective well-being', *Personality and Social Psychology Bulletin*, 11, 1: 89–97.

Enelow, J., and M. J. Hinich (1984) The Spatial Theory of Voting: An Introduction, New York: Cambridge University Press.

Engelen, B. (2007) 'Why compulsory voting can enhance democracy', Acta Politica, 42: 23–39.

Esaiasson, P., and S. Holmberg (1996) *Representation from Above: Members of Parliament and Representative Democracy in Sweden*, Aldershot: Dartmouth.

Evans, G., and S. Whitefield (1998) 'The structuring of political cleavages in post-communist societies: The case of the Czech Republic and Slovakia', *Political Studies*, 46, 1: 115–139.

Eysenck H. J. (1954) *The Psychology of Politics*, London: Routledge and Kegan Paul.

Ezrow, L. (2008) 'Parties' policy programmess and the dog that didn't bark: No evidence that proportional systems promote extreme party positioning', *British Journal of Political Science*, 38, 3: 479–497.

Ezrow, L., and G. Xezonakis (2011) 'Citizen satisfaction with democracy and parties' policy offerings: A cross-national analysis of twelve European party systems, 1976–2003', *Comparative Political Studies*, 44, 9: 1152–1178.

Feather, N. T. (1982) 'Actions in relation to expected consequences: An overview of a research program', in N. T. Feather (ed.), Expectations and Actions: Expectancy-Value Models in Psychology, Hillsdale, NJ: Erlbanm.

Feng, Y. (1997) 'Democracy, political stability and economic growth', *British Journal of Political Science*, 27, 3: 391–418.

Ferejohn, J. (1986) 'Incumbent performance and electoral control', *Public Choice*, 50: 5–26.

Fiske, S. T., and S. E. Taylor (1991) *Social Cognition* (2nd ed.), New York: McGraw-Hill.

Flavin, P., and M. J. Keane (2012) 'Life satisfaction and political participation: Evidence from the United States', Journal of Happiness Studies, 13, 1: 63–78.

Frey, B. S., and A. Stutzer (2000) 'Happiness, economy and institutions', *Economic Journal*, 110: 918–938.

Frey, B. S., and A. Stutzer (2002) 'What can economists learn from happiness research?', *Journal of Economic Literature*, 40, 2: 402–435.

Fromm, E. (1964) *The Heart of Man: Its Genius for Good and Evil.* New York: Harper & Row.

Fuchs, D., and H.-D. Klingemann (1989) 'The left-right schema', in M. K. Jennings and J. van Deth (eds.), *Continuities in Political Action*, Berlin: de Gruyter.

Gabel, M. J., and J. D. Huber (2000) 'Putting parties in their place: Inferring party left-right ideological positions from party manifesto data', *American Journal of Political Science*, 44, 1: 94–103.

Gerber, A. S., and D. P. Green (2000) 'The effects of canvassing, telephone calls, and direct mail on voter turnout: A field experiment', American Political Science Review, 94, 3: 653–663.

Gibson, J. (1989) 'Understandings of justice: Institutional legitimacy, procedural justice, and political tolerance', *Law & Society Review*, 23: 469–496.

Giles, M. W., and M. K. Dantico (1982) 'Political participation and neighborhood social context revisited', *American Journal of Political Science*, 26, 1: 144–150.

Goeree, J. K., and C. A. Holt (2005) 'An explanation of anomalous behavior in models of political participation', *American Political Science Review*, 99, 2: 201–213.

Golder, M., and G. Lloyd (2014) 'Re-evaluating the relationship between electoral rules and ideological congruence', *European Journal of Political Research*, 53, 1: 200–212.

Golder, M., and J. Stramski (2010) 'Ideological congruence and electoral institutions', *American Journal of Political Science*, 54, 1: 90–106.

Gould, C. C. (1988) Rethinking Democracy, Cambridge, UK: Cambridge University Press.

Graham, C., and S. Pettinato (2001) 'Happiness, markets, and democracy: Latin America in comparative perspective', *Journal of Happiness Studies*, 2, 3: 237–268.

Grant, J. T., and T. J. Rudolph (2002) 'To give or not to give: Modeling individuals' contribution decisions', *Political Behavior*, 24, 1: 31–54.

Greenberg, J., and E. Jonas (2003) 'Psychological motives and political orientation – the left, the right, and the rigid: Comments on Jost et al. (2003)', *Psychological Bulletin*, 129, 3: 376–382.

Grundy, K. W., and M. A. Weinstein (1974) *The Ideologies of Violence*, Columbus, Ohio: Charles Merrill.

Gurr, T. R. (1970) *Why Men Rebel*, Princeton, NJ: Princeton University Press.

Hammond, K. R., and D. A. Summers (1965) 'Cognitive dependence on linear and nonlinear cues', *Psychological Review*, 72: 215–224.

Hastie, R., and R. M. Dawes (2010) *Rational Choice in an Uncertain World: The Psychology of Judgment and Decision Making*, Los Angeles: Sage.

Helliwell, J. F. (2003) 'How's life? Combining individual and national variables to explain subjective well-being', *Economic Modelling*, 20: 331–360.

Helliwell, J. F. (2006) 'Well-being, social capital and public policy: What's new?' *Economic Journal*, 116, C34-C45

Helliwell, J. F., and H. Huang (2008) 'How's your government? International evidence linking good governance and well-being', *British Journal of Political Science*, 38, 4: 595–619.

Henderson, A. (2004) 'Satisfaction with democracy: Evidence from Westminster systems', Paper presented at the *Canadian Political Science Association Annual Conference*, Winnipeg, June.

Hinich, M., and M. Munger (1992) 'The spatial theory of ideology', *Journal of Theoretical Politics*, 4: 5–27.

Hix, S., and Hae-Won Jun (2009) 'Party Behaviour in the Parliamentary Arena', *Party Politics*, 15, 6: 667–94.

Hix, S., A. Noury, and G. Roland (2005) 'Power to the parties: cohesion and competition in the European Parliament, 1979–2001', *British Journal of Political Science*, 35, 2: 209–234.

Holm, J. D., and J. P. Robinson (1978) 'Ideological identification and the American voter', *Public Opinion Quarterly*, 42, 2: 235–246.

Holmberg, S. (1997) 'Dynamic opinion representation', *Scandinavian Political Studies*, 20, 3: 265–283.

Horowitz, S., K. Hoff, and B. Milanovic (2009) 'Government turnover: Concepts, measures and applications', *European Journal of Political Research*, 48, 1: 107–129.

Huber, J., and R. Inglehart (1995) 'Expert interpretations of party space and party locations in 42 societies', *Party Politics*, 1, 1: 73–111.

Huber, J. D., and G. B. Powell (1994) 'Congruence between citizens and policy makers in two visions of liberal democracy', *World Politics*, 47: 291–326.

Huckfeldt, R.R. (1979) 'Political participation and the neighborhood social context', American Journal of Political Science, 23, 3: 579–592.

Huckfeldt, R.R., and J. Sprague (1992) 'Political parties and electoral mobilization structure, social structure, and the party canvass', American Political Science Review, 86, 1: 70–86.

Inglehart, R., and H.-D. Klingemann (1976) 'Party identification, ideological preference and the left-right dimension among Western mass publics', in I. Budge, I. Crewe, and D. Farlie (eds.), *Party Identification and Beyond*. London: John Wiley.

Inglehart, R., and H.-D. Klingemann (1979) 'Ideological conceptualization and value priorities', in S.H. Barnes and M. Kaase (eds.), *Political Action: Mass Participation in Five Western Democracies*, Beverly Hills: Sage.

Inglehart, R. (1990) *Culture Shift in Advanced Industrial Society*, Princeton, NJ: Princeton University Press.

Inglehart, R. (1997) Modernization and Postmodernization: Cultural, Economic, and Political Change in 43 Societies, Princeton, NJ: Princeton University Press.

Jackman, R.W. (1987) 'Political institutions and voter turnout in the industrial democracies', American Political Science Review, 81, 2: 405–424.

Jessee, S.A. (2010) 'Partisan bias, political information and spatial voting in the 2008 presidential election', *Journal of Politics*, 72, 2: 327–340.

Jones-Correa, M.A., and D.L. Leal (2001) 'Political participation: Does religion matter?' *Political Research Quarterly*, 54, 4: 751–770.

Jost, J.T., J. Glaser, A.W. Kruglanski, and F.J. Sulloway (2003) 'Political conservatism as motivated social cognition', *Psychological Bulletin*, 129, 3: 339–375.

Jost, J.T., J.L. Napier, H. Thorisdottir, S.D. Gosling, T.P. Palfai, and B. Ostafin (2007) 'Are needs to manage uncertainty and threat associated with political conservatism or ideological extremity?' Personality and Social Psychology Bulletin, 33: 989–1007.

Kaase, M. (1990) 'Mass participation', in K.M. Jennings, J.W. van Deth, D. Fuchs, F.J. Heunks, R. Inglehart, M. Kaase, H.-D. Klingemann, and J.J. Thomassen (eds.), *Continuities in Political Action. A Longitudinal Study of Political Orientations in Three Western Democracies*, Berlin/New York: de Gruyter.

Kaase, M. (1994) 'Is there personalization in politics? Candidates and voting behavior in Germany', *International Political Science Review*, 15, 3: 211–230.

Kahneman, D., and J. Riis (2005) 'Living and thinking about it: Two perspectives on life', in F.A. Huppert, N. Baylis, and B. Keverne (eds.), *The Science of Well-Being*, New York: Oxford University Press.

Karp, J.A., and S.A. Banducci (2008) 'When politics is not just a man's game: Women's representation and political engagement', Electoral Studies, 27, 1: 105–115.

Karp, J.A., S.A. Banducci, and S. Bowler (2008) 'Getting out the vote: party mobilization in a comparative perspective', British Journal of Political Science, 38, 1: 91–112.

Kaufmann, D., and A. Kraay (2002) 'Growth without governance', *Policy Research Working Paper* Series 2928, The World Bank.

Kaufmann, D., A. Kraay, and P. Zoido (2002) *Governance Matters II: Updated Indicators for 2000/01*, Washington DC: World Bank.

Keefer, P. (2013) *DPI2012 Database of Political Institutions: Changes and Variable Definitions*, Washington DC: World Bank.

Keefer, P., and D. Stasavage (2003) 'The limits of delegation: veto players, central bank independence and the credibility of monetary policy', *American Political Science Review*, 97, 3: 407–423.

Kemmelmeier, M. (2008) 'Is there a relationship between political orientation and cognitive ability? A test of three hypotheses in two studies', *Personality and Individual Differences*, 45, 8: 767–772.

Kenny, C. B. (1992) 'Political participation and effects from the social environment', American Journal of Political Science, 36, 1: 259–267.

Kim, I. C. (2005) 'A sense of alienation towards government – an analytic framework', *International Review of Public Administration*, 9, 2: 55–64.

Klandermans, B. (1984) 'Mobilization and participation: Social-psychological expansions of resource mobilization theory', American Sociological Review, 49: 583–600.

Klingemann, H.-D. (1979) 'Ideological conceptualization and political action', in S. H. Barnes and M. Kaase (eds.), Political Action, Beverly Hills: Sage.

Klingemann, H.-D. (1999) 'Mapping political support in the 1990s: A global analysis', in P. Norris (ed.), *Critical Citizens: Global Support for Democratic Governance*, Oxford, UK: Oxford University Press.

Klingemann, H.-D., R. Hofferbert, and I. Budge (1994) *Parties, Policies, and Democracy*, Boulder, CO: Westview Press.

Klingemann, H.-D., A. Volkens, J. L. Bara, I. Budge, and M. D. McDonald (2006) *Mapping Policy Preferences II: Estimates for Parties, Electors, and Governments in Eastern Europe, European Union and OECD 1990–2003*, Oxford, UK: Oxford University Press.

Knutsen, O. (1997) 'The partisan and the value-based component of left-right self-placement: A comparative study', *International Political Science Review* 18, 2: 191–225.

Knutsen, O. (1999) 'Left–Right party polarization among the mass publics', in H. M. Narud and T. Aalberg (eds.), *Challenges to Representative Democracy*, Bergen, Sweden: Fagbokforlaget.

Kolenikov, S., and G. Angeles. (2004) 'The use of discrete data in PCA: Theory, simulations, and applications to socioeconomic indices', Working paper WP-04–85. MEASURE/Evaluation project, Carolina Population Center, University of North Carolina, Chapel Hill.

Konow, J., and J. Earley (2008) 'The Hedonistic Paradox: Is *homo economicus* Happier?' *Journal of Public Economics*, 92, 1–2: 1–33.

Kornberg, A., and H. D. Clarke (1994) 'Beliefs about democracy and satisfaction with democratic government: The Canadian case', *Political Research Quarterly*, 47, 3: 537–563.

Krämer, J., and H. Rattinger (1997) 'The proximity and directional theories of issue voting: Comparative results for the USA and Germany', *European Journal of Political Research*, 32, 1: 1–29.

Kreps, D. M. (1990) *A Course in Microeconomic Theory*, New York: Harvester Wheatsheaf.

Kroh, M. (2007) 'Measuring left-right political orientation: The choice of response format', *Public Opinion Quarterly*, 71, 2: 204–220.

Kuklinksi, J. H., and N. L. Hurley (1994) 'On hearing and interpreting political messages: A cautionary tale of citizen cue-taking', *Journal of Politics*, 56, 3: 729–751.

Laponce, J. A. (1981) *Left and Right the Topography of Political Perceptions*, Toronto: University of Toronto Press.

Laver, M. (2006) 'Legislatures and parliaments', in B. R. Weingast and D. A. Wittman (eds.), *The Oxford Handbook of Political Economy*. New York: Oxford University Press.

Laver, M., and I. Budge (eds.) (1992) Party Policy and Government Coalitions. New York: St. Martin's Press.

Laver, M., and W. Hunt (1992) Policy and Party Competition, London: Routledge.

Lavine, H. (2001) 'The electoral consequences of ambivalence toward presidential candidates', *American Journal of Political Science*, 45, 4: 915–929.

Layard, R. (2006) 'Happiness and public policy: A challenge to the profession', *Economic Journal*, 116, C24–C33.

Leighley, J. E. (1995) 'Attitudes, opportunities, and incentives: A field essay on political participation', Political Research Quarterly, 48, 1: 181–209.

Lewis-Beck, M., and M. Stegmaier (2000) 'Economic determinants of electoral outcomes', *Annual Review of Political Science*, 3: 183–219.

Lijphart, A. (1999) *Patterns of Democracy: Government Forms and Performance in Thirty-Six Countries*, New Haven, CT: Yale University Press.

Linde, J., and J. Ekman (2003) 'Satisfaction with democracy: A note on a frequently used indicator in comparative politics', *European Journal of Political Research*, 42, 3: 391–408.

Lipset, S. M. (1960) Political Man: The Social Bases of Politics, New York: Doubleday.

Lipset, S. M., and W. Schneider (1987) The Confidence Gap: Business, Labor, and Government in the Public Mind. Baltimore: Johns Hopkins University Press.

Listhaug, O., and T. Aalberg (1999) 'Comparative public opinion on distributive justice – Study of equality ideals and attitudes toward current policies', *International Journal of Comparative Sociology*, 40, 1: 117–140.

Luttbeg, N. (1974) *Public opinion and public policy: Models of political linkage*, Homewood, Illinois: Dorsey Press.

Macdonald, S. E., O. Listhaug, and G. Rabinowitz (1991) 'Issues and party support in multiparty systems', *American Political Science Review*, 85, 4: 1107–1131.

Maier, J. (2011) 'The impact of political scandals on the political support: An experimental test of two theories', *International Political Science Review*, 32, 4: 283–302.

Malahy, L. W., M. A. Rubinlicht, and C. R. Kaiser (2009) 'justifying inequality: a cross-temporal investigation of U.S. income disparities and just-world beliefs from 1973 to 2006', *Social Justice Research*, 22, 4: 369–383.

Marien, S., M. Hooghe, and E. Quintelier (2010) 'Inequalities in non-institutionalised forms of political participation: a multi-level analysis of 25 countries', *Political Studies*, 58, 1: 187–213.

Martín, I., and J. W. van Deth (2007) 'Political Involvement', in J. W. van Deth, J. R. Montero, and A. Westholm (eds.), *Citizenship and Involvement in European Democracies: A Comparative Analysis*, London: Routledge.

Marwell, G., and R. E. Ames (1979) 'Experiments on the provision of public goods. I. resources, interest, group size, and the free-rider problem', *American Journal of Sociology*, 84: 1335–1360.

Mattes, R., and M. Bratton (2007) 'Learning about democracy in Africa: Awareness, performance, and experience', *American Journal of Political Science*, 51, 1: 192–217.

McAdam, D., and R. Paulsen (1993) 'Specifying the relationship between social ties and activism', *American Journal of Sociology*, 99: 640–667.

McAllister, I., and S. White (2007) 'Political parties and democratic consolidation in post-communist societies', *Party Politics*, 13, 2: 197–216.

McClosky, H., and D. Chong (1985) 'Similarities and differences between left-wing and right-wing radicals', *British Journal of Political Science*, 15, 3: 329–363.

McDonald, M. D., and I. Budge (2005) *Elections, Parties, Democracy: Conferring the Median Mandate*, New York: Oxford University Press.

McDonnell, D., and J. L. Newell (2011) 'Outsider parties in government in Western Europe', *Party Politics*, 17, 4: 443–452.

McKennell, A. C., and F. M. Andrews (1980) 'Models of cognitive and affect in perceptions of well-being' *Social Indicators Research*, 8, 3: 257–298.

Mebs, K., and N. Nevitte (2002) 'Authority orientations and political support: A cross-national analysis of satisfaction with governments and democracy', *Comparative Sociology*, 1, 3–4: 387–412.

Memoli, V. (2011) 'Government, scandals and political support in Italy', *Interdisciplinary Political Studies*, 1, 2.

Merrill, S., and B. Grofman (1997) 'Directional and proximity models of voter utility and choice: A new synthesis and an illustrative test of competitive models', *Journal of Theoretical Politics*, 9, 1: 25–48.

Milanovic, B., K. Hoff, and S. Horowitz (2008) 'Political alternation as a restraint on investing in influence', *Policy Research Working Paper*, 4747, World Bank.

Milbrath, L.W. (1965) *Political Participation*, Chicago: Rand McNally.

Milbrath, L. W., and L. M. Goel (1977) *Political Participation. How and Why do People Engage in Politics?* Chicago: Rand McNally.

Miller, A. H., and O. Listhaug (1990) 'Political parties and confidence in government: A comparison of Norway, Sweden and United States', *British Journal of Political Science*, 20, 3: 357–386.

Miller, A. H., P. Gurin, G. Gurin, and O. Malanchuk (1981) 'Group consciousness and political participation', *American Journal of Political Science*, 25, 3: 494–511.

Miller, W. E., and D. E. Stokes (1963) 'Constituency influence in Congress', *American Political Science Review*, 57, 1: 45–56.

Miller, W. E., M. K. Jennings, and B. G. Farah (1986) *Parties in Transition: A Longitudinal Study of Party Elites and Party Supporters*. New York: Russell Sage Foundation.

Moehler, D. C. (2009) 'Critical citizens and submissive subjects: Election losers and winners in Africa', *British Journal of Political Science*, 39, 2: 345–366.

Montero, J. R., and R. Gunther (1994) 'Democratic legitimacy in Spain', Paper presented at the *IPSA World Congress*, Berlin.

Morrow, J. D. (1994) *Game Theory for Political Scientists*, Princeton, NJ: Princeton University Press.

Mughan, A. (2000) *Media and the Presidentialization of Parliamentary Elections*, London: Palgrave.

Muller, E. N. (1979) 'Aggressive political participation', *Academy of Political Science*, 95: 689–691.

Nadeau, R., and A. Blais (1993) 'Accepting the election outcome: The effect of participation on losers' consent', *British Journal of Political Science*, 23, 4: 553–563.

Napier, J. L., and J. T. Jost (2008) 'Why are conservatives happier than liberals?' *Psychological Science*, 19, 6: 565–572.

Nexon, D. (1971) 'Asymmetry in the political system: Occasional activists in the Republican and Democratic parties, 1956–1964', American Political Science Review, 65, 3: 716–730.

Nie, N. H., B. G. Powell, and P. Kenneth (1969) 'Social structure and political participation', *American Political Science Review*, 63, 3: 808–832.

Norris, P. (ed.) (1999) *Critical Citizens: Global Support for Democratic Governance*, Oxford, UK: Oxford University Press.

Norris, P. (2006) 'Support for democratic governance: Multidimensional concept and survey measures', Paper for the LAPOP-UNDP workshop on *Candidate Indicators for the UNDP Democracy Support Index (DSI)*. Center for the Americas at Vanderbilt University, Nashville, May 5–6, p. 6.

Norris, P. (2014) *Why Electoral Integrity Matters*, New York: Cambridge University Press

Norris, P., S. Walgrave, and P. Van Aelst (2005) 'Who demonstrates? Antistate rebels, conventional participants, or everyone?' *Comparative politics*, 37, 2: 189–205.

Nye, J. S., P. D. Zelikow, and D. C. King (1997) *Why People Don't Trust Government*, Cambridge, MA: Harvard University Press.

Olson, M. (1965) *The Logic of Collective Action*, Cambridge, MA: Harvard University Press.

Opp, K.-D. (1986) 'Soft incentives and collective action: Participation in the anti-nuclear movement', *British Journal of Political Science*, 16, 1: 87–112.

Opp, K.-D., and C. Gern (1993) 'Dissident groups, personal networks, and spontaneous cooperation. The East German revolution of 1989', *American Sociological Review*, 58: 659–680.

Opp, K.-D., S. E. Finkel, E. N. Muller, G. Wolfsfeld, H. A. Dietz, and J. D. Green (1995) 'Left-right ideology and collective political action: A comparative analysis of Germany, Israel, and Peru', in C. J. Jenkings and B. Klandermans (eds.), *The Politics of Social Protest: Comparative Perspectives on States and Social Movements*, Minneapolis: University of Minnesota Press.

Orit, K. (2005) 'When moderate voters prefer extreme parties: Policy balancing in parliamentary elections', *American Political Science Review*, 99, 2: 185–199.

Ott, J. C. (2010) 'Good governance and happiness in nations: Technical quality precedes democracy and quality beats size', *Journal of Happiness Studies*, 11, 3: 353–368.

Ovaska, T., and R. Takashima (2006) 'Economic policy and level of self-perceived well-being. An international comparison', *The Journal of Socio-Economics*, 35: 308–325.

Pacek, A., and B. Radcliff (2008) 'Assessing the welfare state: The politics of happiness', *Perspectives on Politics*, 6, 2: 267–277.

Palfrey, T. R., and H. Rosenthal (1985) 'Voter participation and strategic uncertainty', *American Political Science Review*, 79, 1: 62–78.

Pitkin, H. F. (1967) *The Concept of Representation*, Berkeley: University of California Press.

Policzer, P. (2000) 'Review of patterns of democracy: Government forms and performance in thirty-six countries', *Canadian Journal of Political Science*, 33: 837–838.

Poole, K. (2005) *Spatial Models of Parliamentary Voting*, Cambridge, UK: Cambridge University Press.

Powell, G. B. (2000) *Elections as Instruments of Democracy*, New Haven, CT: Yale University Press.

Powell G. B. (2005) 'The chain of responsiveness', in L. Diamond and L. Morlino, *Assessing the Quality of Democracy*, Baltimore: The Johns Hopkins University Press.

Powell, G. B., and G. Vanberg (2000) 'Election laws, disproportionality and median correspondence: Implications for two visions of democracy', *British Journal of Political Science*, 30, 3: 383–411.

Putnam, R. D. (1993) *Making Democracy Work. Civic Traditions in Modern Italy*, Princeton: Princeton University Press.

Rabe-Hesketh, S., and Skrondal A. (2008) *Multilevel and Longitudinal Modeling Using Stata*, Second Edition, Texas: Stata Press.

Rabinowitz, G., and S. E. Macdonald (1989) 'A directional theory of voting', *American Political Science Review*, 83, 1: 93–121.

Radcliff, B. (2001) 'Politics, markets, and life satisfaction: The political economy of human happiness', *American Political Science Review*, 95, 4: 939–952.

Rahn, W. M. (1993) 'The role of partisan stereotypes in information processing about political candidates', *American Journal of Political Science*, 37, 2: 472–496.

Raudenbush, S. W., and A. S. Bryk (2002) *Hierarchical Lineal Models*. London: Sage.

Ray, L., and H. M. Narud (2000) 'Mapping the Norwegian political space: Some findings from an expert survey', *Party Politics*, 6, 2: 225–239.

Reher, S. (2013) 'The heuristic value of priorities: How political sophistication moderates the effects of policy representation on satisfaction with democracy', Paper presented at the 7th Annual Conference of the Midwest Political Science Association (MPSA), Chicago, April 11–14.

Riker, W. (1982) Liberalism Against Populism: *A Confrontation Between the Theory of Democracy and the Theory of Social Choice*, Prospect Heights, NY: Waveland Press.

Riker, W., and P. C. Ordeshook (1968) 'A theory of the calculus of voting', American Political Science Review, 62: 25–42.

Rokeach M. (1960) *The Open and Closed Mind*. New York: Basic Books.

Rosenstone, S. J., and J. M. Hansen (1993) *Mobilization, Participation, and Democracy in America*. New York: Macmillan.

Sani, G. (1974) 'A test of the least-distance model of voting choice Italy, 1972', *Comparative Political Studies*, 7, 2: 193–208.

Sani, G., and G. Sartori (1983) 'Polarization, fragmentation and competition', in H. Daalder and P. Mair (eds.), *Western European Party Systems*, London: Sage.

Sartori, G. (1976) *Parties and Party Systems. A Framework for Analysis*, Cambridge, UK: Cambridge University Press.

Schyns, P. (1998) 'Crossnational difference in happiness: Economic and cultural factor explored', *Social Indicators Research*, 43, 1–2: 3–26.

Schyns, P. (2002) 'Wealth of nations, individual income and life satisfaction in 42 countries: A multilevel approach', *Social Indicators Research*, 60, 1–3: 5–40.

Schumpeter, J. A. (1942) *Capitalism, Socialism and Democracy*, New York: Harper and Brothers.

Scott, J., and H. Schuman (1988) 'Attitude strength and social action in the abortion dispute', American Sociological Review, 53: 785–793.

Shils, E. A. (1954) 'Authoritarianism: Right and left', in R. Christie and M. Jahoda (eds.), *Studies in the Scope and Method of the Authoritarian Personality*, Glencoe, IL: Free Press.

Sidanius, J. (1985) 'Cognitive functioning and sociopolitical ideology revisited', *Political Psychology*, 6, 4: 637–661.

Sigelman, L., and S. N. Yough (1978) 'Left–right polarization in national party systems: A cross-national analysis', *Comparative Political Studies*, 11, 3: 355–379.

Simon, H. A. (1985) 'Human nature in politics: The dialogue of psychology with political science', American Political Science Review, 79, 2: 293–304.

Singh, S. (2014). 'Linear and quadratic utility loss functions in voting behavior research', *Journal of Theoretical Politics*, 26, 1: 35–58.

Snyder, J. M. Jr., and T. Groseclose (2001) 'Estimating party influence in congressional roll-call voting', *American Journal of Political Science*, 44, 2: 193–211.

Soroka, S. N., and C. Wlezien (2010) *Degrees of Democracy: Politics, Public Opinion, and Policy*, Cambridge, UK: Cambridge University Press.

Steenbergen, M. R., and B. S. Jones (2002) 'Modeling multilivel data structures', *American Journal of Political Science*, 46, 1: 218–237.

Steenbergen, M. R., and G. Marks (2007) 'Evaluating expert judgments', *European Journal of Political Research*, 46, 3: 347–366.

Stimson, J. A. (1976) 'Public support for American presidents: A cyclical model', *Public Opinion Quarterly*, 40, 1: 1–21.

Stimson, J. A., M. B. MacKuen, and R. S. Erikson (1995) 'Dynamic representation', *American Political Science Review*, 89, 3: 543–565.

Stokes, D. E. (1963) 'Spatial models of party competition', *American Political Science Review*, 57, 2: 368–77.

Suh, E., E. Diener, S. Oishi, and H. C. Triandis (1998) 'The shifting basis of life satisfaction judgments across cultures: Emotions versus norms', *Journal of Personality and Social Psychology*, 74, 2: 482–493.

Svolik, M. (2008) 'Authoritarian reversal and democratic consolidation', *American Political Science Review*, 102, 2: 153–168.

Tavits, M. (2008) 'Representation, corruption, and subjective well-being', *Comparative Political Studies*, 41, 12: 1607–1630.

Taylor, P., C. Funk, and P. Craighill (2006) *Are We Happy Yet?* Washington, DC: Pew Research Center.

Teorell, J. (2006) 'Political participation and three theories of democracy: A research inventory and agenda', *European Journal of Political Research*, 45, 5: 787–810.

Thomassen, J.J.A. (1994) 'Empirical research into political representation: Failing democracy or failing models?', in M. K. Jennings and T. E. Mann (eds.), *Elections at Home and Abroad*, Ann Arbor: The University of Michigan Press.

Thomassen, J.J.A. (1999) 'Political communication between political elites and mass publics: The role of belief systems', in W. Miller, R. Pierce, J.J.A. Thomassen, R. Herrera, S. Holmberg, P. Esaiasson, and B. Wessels (eds.), *Policy Representation in Western Democracies*, Oxford, UK: Oxford University Press.

Thomassen, J.J.A., and H. Schmitt (1997) 'Policy representation', *European Journal of Political Research*, 32, 2: 165–184.

Thompson, J. B. (2000) *Political Scandals: Power and Visibility in the Media Age.* Cambridge, UK: Blackwell.

Thurner, P. W., and A. Eymann (2000) 'Policy-specific alienation and indifference in the calculus of voting: A simultaneous model of party choice and abstention', *Public Choice*, 102, 1: 49–75.

Tomkins, S. S. (1963) 'Left and right: A basic dimension of ideology and personality', in R. W. White (ed.), *The Study of Lives: Essays in Honor of Henry A. Murray*, Chicago: Aldine-Atherton.

Triandis, H. C. (1995) *Individualism and Collectivism*, Boulder, CO: Westview Press.

Tsebelis, G. (2002). *Veto Players. How Political Institutions Work.* Princeton: Princeton University Press.

Tyler, T. (1990) *Why People Follow the Law: Procedural Justice, Legitimacy, and Compliance*, New Haven, CT: Yale University Press.

van der Meer, T., J. W. van Deth, and P. Scheepers (2009) 'The politicized participant: Ideology and political action in 20 democracies', *Comparative Political Studies*, 42, 11: 1426–1457.

Veenhoven, R. (1984) *Conditions of Happiness.* Dordrecht, The Netherlands: Reidel.

Veenhoven, R. (1993). *Happiness in Nations: Subjective Appreciation of Life in 56 Nations, 1946–1992.* Rotterdam: Erasmus University of Rotterdam.

Veenhoven, R. (1995) 'The cross-national pattern of happiness: Test of predictions implied in three theories of happiness', *Social Indicators Research*, 34, 1: 33–68.

Veenhoven, R. (2000) 'Well-being in the welfare state: Level not higher, distribution not more equitable', *Journal of Comparative Policy Analysis*, 2, 1: 91–125.

Verba, S., and R. Brody (1970) 'Participation policy preferences, and the war in Vietnam', *Public Opinion Quarterly*, 34, 3: 325–332.

Verba, S., and N. H. Nie (1972) *Participation in America: Political Democracy and Social Equality*, New York: Harper and Row.

Verba, S., N. H. Nie, and J. Kim (1978) *Participation and Political Equality: A Seven-Nation Comparison*, New York: Cambridge University Press.

Verba, S., K.L. Schlozman, and H. Brady (1995) *Voice and Equality: Civic Voluntarism in American Politics*, Cambridge, MA: Harvard University Press.

Verba, S., K. L. Schlozman, and H. Brady, and N. H. Nie (1993) 'Race, ethnicity and political resources: Participation in the United States', *British Journal of Political Science*, 23, 4: 453–497.

Wagner, A. F., M. Dufour, and F. Schneider (2003) 'Satisfaction not guaranteed: Institutions and satisfaction with democracy in Western Europe', *CESifo* Working paper n. 910.

Wagner, A. F., F. G. Schneider, and M. Halla (2009) 'The quality of institutions and satisfaction with democracy in Western Europe: A panel analysis', *European Journal of Political Economy*, 25: 30–41.

Waldron-Moore, P. (1999) 'Eastern Europe at the crossroads of democratic transition: Evaluating support for democratic institutions, satisfaction with democratic government, and consolidation of democratic regimes', *Comparative Political Studies*, 32, 1: 32–62.

Warwick, P. G. (1994) *Government Survival in Parliamentary Democracies*, Cambridge, UK: Cambridge University Press.

Warwick, P. V. (2001) 'Coalition policy in parliamentary democracies: Who gets how much and why', *Comparative Political Studies*, 34, 10: 1212–1236.

Wells, J. M., and J. Krieckhaus (2006) 'Does national context influence democratic satisfaction? A multi-level analysis', *Political Research Quarterly*, 59, 4: 69–578.

Wessels, B., and H. Schmitt (2008) 'Meaningful choices, political supply, and institutional effectiveness', *Electoral Studies*, 27, 1: 19–30.

West, D. M. (1988) 'Activists and economic policymaking in congress', *American Journal of Political Science*, 32, 3: 662–680.

'What's gone wrong with democracy'. (2014, March 1). *The Economist*, Available at http://www.economist.com/news/essays/21596796-democracy-was-most-successful-political-idea-20th-century-why-has-it-run-trouble-and-what-can-be-do.

Wheeler, R. J. (1991) 'The theoretical and empirical structure of general well-being', *Social Indicators Research*, 24, 1: 71–79.

Whiteley, P., H. D. Clarke, D. Sanders, and M. C. Stewart (2010) 'Government performance and life satisfaction in contemporary Britain', *Journal of Politics*, 72, 3: 733–746.

Wiesehomeier, N., and K. Benoit (2009) 'Presidents, parties, and policy competition', *Journal of Politics*, 71, 4: 1435–1447.

Wooldridge, J. M. (2003) 'Cluster-sample methods in applied econometrics', *American Economic Review*, 93: 133–138.

World Bank (2014) *The Worldwide Governance Indicators (WGI) project World Bank*. Available at http://info.worldbank.org/governance/wgi/index.aspx#home.

Zechmeister, E. J. (2006) 'What's left and who's right? A q-method study of individual and contextual influences on the meaning of ideological labels', *Political Behavior*, 28, 2: 151–173.

Index

For Product Safety Concerns and Information please contact our EU
representative GPSR@taylorandfrancis.com
Taylor & Francis Verlag GmbH, Kaufingerstraße 24, 80331 München, Germany

www.ingramcontent.com/pod-product-compliance
Ingram Content Group UK Ltd.
Pitfield, Milton Keynes, MK11 3LW, UK
UKHW020946180425
457613UK00019B/551